EVERYDAY LIFE IN

BABYLONIA
& ASSYRIA

1 Babylon, from in front of the Ishtar Gate, in the time of King Nebuchadnezzar II
A reconstruction by E. Unger

EVERYDAY LIFE IN
BABYLONIA
& ASSYRIA

H. W. F. SAGGS

Drawings by Helen Nixon Fairfield

DORSET PRESS
New York

First published by B. T. Batsford 1965

This edition published by Dorset Press,
a division of Marboro Books Corporation,
by arrangement with B. T. Batsford Ltd
1987 Dorset Press

ISBN 0-88029-127-3

Printed in the United States of America
M 9 8 7 6 5 4 3 2 1

Preface

THE way of life with which this book deals flourished for 2000 years of the most formative period of human history, and it would require far more than the space available even to touch upon every significant aspect of this subject. I have therefore had to confine myself to a more modest task. What I have attempted has been to give an introduction to the subject by a sketch of Babylonian and Assyrian life at a few key-points, seen in the context of the historical setting.

I need hardly point out to my professional colleagues that this book is not written for them; therefore, if, in using the original sources, I have chosen, for the sake of English idiom, to translate a singular by a plural, or to alter a tense, I trust they will not turn and rend me. My main purpose will be served if I succeed in convincing some of my readers, amongst the many now interested in the ancient world, that Babylonian and Assyrian civilisation is not wholly alien to our own.

Although I have been able in many cases to suggest sources for illustrations, the credit and responsibility for the final selection and treatment of the illustrations belong, not to me as author, but to the talented artist, Mrs H. Fairfield, and to Mr P. Kemmis Betty.

H. W. F. SAGGS

Contents

The Illustrations

Note—*The italicised numerals in parentheses in the text refer to the figure-numbers of the illustrations*

THE ILLUSTRATIONS

Acknowledgment

The Author and Publishers wish to thank the following for permission to reproduce the illustrations appearing in this book:

The Director-General of Antiquities, Baghdad for figs. 13, 15 and 16
The Trustees of the British Museum for figs. 4, 6, 7, 25, 26, 44, 45, 60, 61, 81 and 83
The British School of Archaeology in Iraq for fig. 23
The Mansell Collection for figs. 24, 46, 47 and 59
Musée du Louvre for figs. 5 and 82
Oriental Institute, University of Chicago for fig. 1
Mrs H. W. F. Saggs for fig. 91
Staatliche Museen, Berlin for figs. 43 and 90
The Times Publishing Company Ltd for fig. 85
Fig. 14 is reproduced from C. R. Woolley, *Ur Excavations II*; fig. 84 from W. Andrae, *Coloured Ceramics from Assur*; fig. 89 from R. Koldewey, *Das Ischtar-Tor in Babylon*.

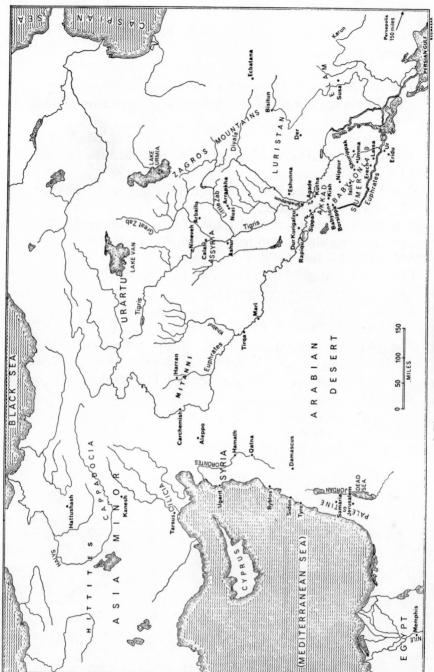

2 The Ancient Near and Middle East

Chapter I

A FORGOTTEN CIVILISATION

For over 2000 years one of the greatest of human achievements, the civilisation of Babylonia and Assyria, lay buried and almost forgotten beneath the soil of the land we now know as Iraq (earlier called Mesopotamia). There remained of it only certain accounts, of doubtful reliability, in Greek literature, together with some Biblical statements, perhaps biased, about the Assyrians, and more dubious traditions of a much earlier period in a land called Shinar. In Shinar, according to the Biblical account, had been built the tower of Babel; here too had lived the sole surviving family of the great Flood, whilst somewhere in this region, at the beginning of man's history, had been the mythical Garden of Eden.

Occasional travellers, attracted by the magic of the names of Babylon and Nineveh, had visited the great ancient mounds of Iraq from the time of the Crusades onwards. Some left accounts of their journeys and their speculations, and even brought back to Europe relics—inscribed bricks and the like—of the ancient cities. The vast ruins of Nineveh, standing across the Tigris from the city of Mosul, had probably never entirely lost their identification in local tradition, and even by European travellers they were recognised for what they were as early as the twelfth century A.D. The site of Babylon, however, remained longer in doubt, though travellers did not hesitate to identify one or other of the gigantic brick structures still standing in South Iraq with the ill-starred tower of Babel. The precise location of Babylon was not definitely known until the seventeenth century.

The first man to make a more scientific examination of the ancient mounds of Iraq was Claudius James Rich. Rich was a young Englishman, with no great advantages of birth, who at the age of twenty-one had risen by his own merits, in particular his linguistic ability, to be the Resident of the East India Company in Baghdad, a post of considerable responsibility and pomp. In 1811 he took the opportunity of paying a visit to Babylon, where in the

17

course of a fruitful ten days he made a survey of the whole great site, and employed workmen to undertake some crude excavations. The resulting collection of inscribed bricks, cuneiform clay tablets and cylinder seals, together with Rich's *Memoir on the Ruins of Babylon*, published in 1812, may properly be taken to mark the beginning of the science of Assyriology. Rich made a second visit some years later, publishing a *Second Memoir on Babylon* (1818). There is a reference to the stir caused by these new discoveries in Byron's lines in *Don Juan*, where the poet speaks of

> . . . *some infidels, who don't*
> *Because they can't, find out the very spot*
> *Of that same Babel, or because they won't*
> (*Though Claudius Rich, Esquire, some bricks has got,*
> *And written lately two memoirs upon't*).

At Rich's premature death from cholera in 1821 his collection of antiquities was sold to the British Museum, where the cuneiform material became the basis of the great Assyriological collection there, now recognised as one of the finest in the world.

Apart from a sounding at Babylon in 1827, after Rich's pioneer work there were no further excavations in Iraq until the 1840s, although travellers continued to visit and record their impressions of the ancient mounds (or *tells*) of the country.

The year 1840 marked the first arrival in Iraq of another young man who in the course of the next eleven years was to put the archaeological side of the new science of Assyriology on a sound foundation. The young man was Henry Austen Layard,* then twenty-three. Layard, who had failed to make good in his uncle's highly respectable firm of solicitors, was on his way over-land to an opening which had been promised for him in Ceylon. Deeply impressed by the ancient mounds of Iraq and fascinated by the life and society of the Near and Middle East in general, he lingered in that area as long as he could and finally abandoned his original intention, not without some anxiety as to his uncle's possible reactions. His knowledge of languages, the charm of his personality, his intelligence and industry, and his courage, endurance, and taste for adventure, had combined to give him considerable first-hand knowledge of Oriental politics, and he now had hopes of a career in the diplomatic service. In this, however,

---

*During part of his life Layard used his Christian names in the order Austen Henry, out of respect to his uncle, a Mr Austen.

3 Ruins of the ziggurrat at Borsippa

he was, through the stubbornness of the Foreign Office, for some years disappointed, even though he managed to be of considerable assistance privately to the British Ambassador in Constantinople. The latter, although unable to obtain early official status for Layard, did give him personal and financial support, and in 1845 encouraged him to undertake excavations at the mound of Nimrud, about twenty miles south of Mosul. Successfully overcoming both official obstruction and financial and practical difficulties, Layard opened up the hidden palaces of one of the Assyrian capitals, not (as he at first supposed) Nineveh, but Calah, mentioned in *Genesis* x 12. He returned to England and published an account of his work in 1849, when it at once created a nationwide sensation.

Layard was not quite first in the field of large-scale excavation in Iraq, for he had an eminent predecessor in the French Consul Paul Botta, who began excavations in 1842. Botta, described by a contemporary as 'a scientific man but a d—d bad consul', was a very good friend to Layard, who before 1845 received much stimulus towards archaeological research by the fact that Botta gave him free access to his own reports as they passed through Constantinople.

Whilst, like Layard, Botta carried out minor archaeological excavations at several places, the site of his principal work was Khorsabad, north-east of Mosul. Both these great pioneers also at different times dug at Kuyunjik, the site of Nineveh itself. All three sites—Khorsabad, Kuyunjik, and Nimrud—turned out to be ruins of capital cities of the period of Assyrian greatness between the ninth and seventh centuries B.C., which coincided largely with the period of the divided kingdoms of Israel and Judah, well known from the Old Testament. It was the sidelights the new discoveries shed upon Biblical history, as well as the striking nature of many of the early finds themselves—colossal winged bulls and lions (4), now impressive features of the British Museum and the Louvre, together with vivid scenes carved in low relief on limestone friezes—which won the immediate interest of the general public of Great Britain and France. It was also the fact that all the main early finds came from Assyria that led to the new science being called 'Assyriology', a name still retained, although it is now recognised that Assyria formed only a part, and not even the most important part, of the whole civilisation concerned.

Winged bulls and limestone friezes, spectacular though they may be, would not by themselves have given us much insight into the civilisation of the people who left these things behind. Fortunately, along with these objects, there were, either carved on the bulls, lions or friezes, or impressed upon cylinders or tablets of clay, inscriptions in unknown characters built up from wedge-shaped (or 'cuneiform') strokes. It was the decipherment of this cuneiform script which ultimately opened up to the modern world the whole of Babylonian and Assyrian thought and life.

A few cuneiform inscriptions had been published long before the excavations of Botta and Layard, and work upon these had provided the key which was to unlock the new material. In the ruins of the palaces of the ancient Persian kings, particularly at Persepolis, are many well-preserved cuneiform inscriptions on stone. Portions of these were copied by a number of travellers as curiosities, but it was not until the late eighteenth century, when more careful and complete copies had been made, that it was noticed that these inscriptions from the Persian palaces contained three different systems of writing (8), and that one of them was the system found on the inscribed bricks from the region of Babylon.

There are basically three different ways in which languages can be committed to writing. The most primitive is to have one sign (called an 'ideogram' or 'logogram') for each word or idea. If such a system is to be of any widespread use, it will obviously require hundreds, if not thousands, of distinct signs. Chinese writing is an

4 Assyrian colossal lion
Limestone statue from the palace at Khorsabad, eighth century B.C.

5 'Stele of the Vultures': Eannatum leading
his soldiers over enemy dead (*above*), and riding
in his chariot (*below*)
Limestone relief, mid-third millennium B.C.

6–7 Cuneiform clay tablet and envelope
From Kuyunjik, seventh century B.C.

example of this. The second possible writing system is to have a separate sign, not for each word, but for each syllable. Since the number of possible syllables in a language is far less than the number of possible words, such a system will require far fewer signs. For ancient Near Eastern languages using this

8 The three scripts from Persepolis
(After C. Niebuhr, 1778)

system of writing the number of syllabic signs needed was not less than a hundred. The third basic method of writing is the one we commonly use, the alphabetic system, in which the principal sounds occurring in a language are each given a separate symbol. The number of symbols will vary slightly from one alphabet to another, according to the sounds commonly occurring in a particular language and the efficiency with which these sounds are distinguished in writing, but almost always the number of symbols in an alphabet will be between twenty and fifty.

In the case of the three scripts from Persepolis, one of them proved to have less than fifty different signs, and so could reasonably be taken as alphabetic. Some of the texts thus taken as alphabetic were short inscriptions carved above the heads of reliefs of figures obviously representing kings, and this suggested that such inscriptions might contain a royal name and titles. A clue to the decipherment was that it was known from later Persian sources that the usual form of the title of the Persian kings was 'So-and-so, the Great King, King of Kings, son of So-and-so'. Working from such data, a German scholar, G. F. Grotefend, was able as early as 1802 to make considerable progress in the decipherment of the alphabetic cuneiform script, assigning correct values to nearly one-third of the alphabet. Between then and the 1830s a number of scholars worked on the script, with varying degrees of success, so that in later years there arose at one time a sharp controversy about who deserved the major credit for the final decipherment. Several scholars certainly took a share in it, but it is clear that a considerable part of the credit is due to yet another young Englishman, Henry Creswicke Rawlinson.

Rawlinson, a good classical scholar and a fine athlete, held an

23

9 The Rock of Bisitun

appointment in the East India Company, and in 1835, at the age of twenty-five, was posted to duties in Persia, about twenty miles from the famous Rock of Bisitun (or Behistun). The Rock of Bisitun, on the main ancient route from Babylon to Ecbatana (the ancient capital of the Medes) rises sheer almost 1700 feet, and on it, about 300 feet up, the ancient Persian king Darius I (522–486 B.C.) had a monument carved showing him overcoming his enemies (9). Accompanying the sculptures were carved inscriptions which (as we now know) were in three languages, Old Persian, Elamite, and Akkadian, in the three scripts already mentioned. Although many people had seen the sculptures and inscriptions from below, these details about the languages in which they were written were of course known to no one when Rawlinson arrived in Persia. He was already interested in the problem of decipherment, and saw in the inscriptions at Bisitun, far longer than the only ones to which scholars had had access up to that time, the most promising material for a complete solution. By climbing up the side of the cliff to a narrow ledge overhanging a drop of over a hundred feet, Rawlinson was able, in the course of several visits during 1836 and 1837, to copy about 200 lines of the particular inscription (now known to be in the language called Old Persian) which was written in the alphabetic script. Rawlinson had already arrived at some of the letters of the Old Persian alphabet by the

24

same kind of method as that employed by Grotefend. The new material enabled Rawlinson to decipher virtually the whole alphabet, and by his knowledge of later languages related to Old Persian he was able by 1839 to give a substantially accurate summary of the meaning of the whole of the 200 lines. Thus the Old Persian script and language had been largely deciphered before 1840.

There still remained the even more difficult task, the decipherment of the scripts and languages of the Elamite and Akkadian versions of the trilingual texts. By 1846 Rawlinson and others had made substantial progress with Elamite, but little was known about Akkadian writing. The credit for the earliest substantial success in the decipherment of Akkadian cuneiform goes to an Irish parson named Edward Hincks. However, others, including Rawlinson, were not far behind, and by 1850 it was possible for these scholars to make out the general sense of Akkadian texts of an historical nature. None the less, the learned world was not fully convinced. For this reason, a test was made in 1856–7, four of the leading scholars, Hincks, Rawlinson, Oppert and Fox Talbot, being set to prepare independent translations of a long newly discovered text. When it was found that the result of the four substantially agreed, there could be no further doubt that the script and language of Akkadian had been deciphered.

The great difficulty in deciphering Akkadian lay not mainly in the language itself, but in the manner of writing it. The script, in its later form, was a mixture of two of the writing systems mentioned above, some of the signs being ideograms and others syllograms (*i.e.* signs denoting syllables). It was further complicated by the fact that some signs could be used either as ideograms or as syllograms, whilst some syllograms might denote several completely different syllables within the same text. Thus the one sign 𒌓 could (at one period and in a single text) be either the ideogram for 'day' or a syllable to be pronounced *ud* or *tu* or *tam* or *par* or *likh* or *khish*. To complicate matters further, several different signs might represent the same syllable: thus either 𒌋 or 𒍦 could occur for the syllable *u* in certain positions in a word.

The initial decipherment of Akkadian was thus no simple matter. However, once this had been achieved, further progress was merely a matter of perseverance and time. It was soon recognised that the writing system could not have been invented for

Akkadian, and, as was expected by some of the pioneers, scholars found amongst the cuneiform inscriptions from Babylonia texts in another language, as different from Akkadian as Turkish is from English. This language, today known as Sumerian (from the race which originally spoke it) has only become well understood in the last forty years, and there is still much dispute about the details of the interpretation of Sumerian texts. Most Akkadian texts, on the other hand, can now be understood as well as the Hebrew of the Old Testament.

Whilst the ancient Sumerians, Babylonians and Assyrians had sometimes carved inscriptions on stone monuments, the usual writing materials consisted of lumps of clay, most commonly of a size to be held in the hand, but frequently larger (43). Layard's critics have alleged that at first he treated such pieces of inscribed clay as merely oddly decorated pottery, but certainly before he left Nimrud in June 1847 he knew what they were. Later, at Kuyunjik, Layard and his successors found, and brought back for the British Museum, the remains of several libraries of cuneiform clay tablets collected by Assyrian kings. The 25,000 fragments concerned still form the most important single collection of cuneiform material known: it is indeed so comprehensive that some Assyriologists, irreverently referred to by their colleagues as 'Kuyunjikologists', are able to make important contributions to research whilst virtually limiting their interests to this particular collection (6, 7).

Layard retired from archaeology in 1851, going into politics, but his work at Kuyunjik and elsewhere, on behalf of the British Museum, was carried on by others. The French had been active in excavation from the beginning, and Germany and America began major excavations in the late 1880s. Many other nations followed suit, and Assyriology, both in its archaeological aspects and in the study of cuneiform material, has become a field in which international co-operation is a reality. There is seldom a year in which there are not three or four expeditions to Iraq from different countries, and at the Rencontre Assyriologique Internationale, held annually, one may meet delegates from Great Britain, America, France, Germany (East and West), Czechoslovakia, Yugoslavia, Russia, Turkey, Finland, Holland, Iraq, Lebanon, Israel, Austria, Belgium, Switzerland, and Denmark, all joined by the desire to deepen knowledge of ancient Mesopotamian civilisation.

A FORGOTTEN CIVILISATION

THE LAND AND RACES OF BABYLONIA AND ASSYRIA

Ancient Babylonia and Assyria covered approximately the region which today is known as Iraq, though some places important in the ancient civilisation are to be found in Turkey and Syria. Iraq is a land which depends for its life, and in part for its physical existence, upon its great rivers, the Euphrates and the Tigris. Without these rivers two-thirds of the country would be an arid desert, whilst it is these rivers which have created, by their silt deposits, the whole region, a great alluvial plain, which extends from about 100 miles north of Baghdad down to the Persian Gulf. This alluvial soil can be, under the influence of the sun and adequate irrigation, of astonishingly high fertility, and it was in the alluvial plain that the ancient civilisation had its origin and flowering. East and north of the alluvial plain the land rises into chains of foothills, and finally into mountains of up to 10,000 feet on the borders of Persia and Turkey. To the west of the Euphrates the land merges into the Syrian and Arabian deserts.

It was the southern part of this land, roughly from the latitude of Baghdad, which in ancient times was Babylonia, the northern part being Assyria. The whole is sometimes referred to as Mesopotamia, from the Greek for 'between the rivers', though the Greeks themselves used this term of rather a different area.

The story of Mesopotamian civilisation, and with it the story of our own civilisation, begins a little over 5000 years ago, in the hot swamps of South Iraq. A strange people, the Sumerians, whose precise origin is still unknown, had come (whether by land or sea we are not certain) from somewhere to the east or north-east to settle in the region around the head of the Persian Gulf. This region is deficient in some of the basic materials of civilised existence, such as hard timber, stone, and metal ores, but is rich in three others, namely, sunshine, water, and mud. It was out of mud that the Sumerians built their civilisation, and it is mud, in the form of inscribed clay tablets, which enables us to see back almost to the beginning of the 5000 years which separate us from the original Sumerian settlement.

South Iraq was not empty when the Sumerians arrived. There already existed thriving villages, some of which became the basis of later Sumerian cities. Archaeology shows that the newcomers adopted much of the building, agricultural and irrigational technology of the people already there, though at the same time

27

10 Bowls of the pre-Sumerian period

they introduced or invented other processes and techniques not previously found in the country. It has been suggested that the Sumerians arrived in the land as warlike nomadic shepherds, imposing themselves upon the settled peoples as a ruling caste. Other scholars think that the Sumerians were themselves peasant farmers, perhaps driven from a homeland in Central Asia by climatic changes. The evidence is scanty and ambiguous, and at present not sufficient for us to make a decision.

The characteristic form into which Sumerian society grew was, from early in the third millennium B.C., the walled city at the centre of a small city-state, with a number of dependent villages in the surrounding countryside. It should perhaps be emphasised that the basis of the Sumerian city was agriculture and not industry. The two most prominent features of the Sumerian city were its irrigation system and its main temple built on a terrace. This terrace-temple in course of time developed to become the stepped tower known as the ziggurat (p. 156). The city temple might be of considerable splendour with stone foundations, but most of the human occupants of the city still lived in small mud huts.

In theory the city was the estate of the local deity, whose chief human representative was known as the *En*; this functionary could apparently be either a man or a woman. Originally control of the city-state had been in the hands of all free citizens, who arrived at decisions on major policy in public council. There are always some activities, however, which require on-the-spot decisions, and so the citizens came to appoint a man called the *Ensi* to direct and co-ordinate agricultural operations, whilst in times of crisis they would choose a king (Sumerian *Lugal*, literally 'Big Man') as military leader (5). Although both *Ensi* and *Lugal* were originally elected, once a man had been appointed there would be a strong tendency for his position to become permanent and hereditary, and also for the various leading positions in the city-state to be gathered into one person. Thus the famous Gilgamesh of Erech (p. 87) was both *En* and *Lugal*, and a number of other Sumerian rulers were both *Lugal* and *Ensi*. As a result the original democratic organisation gave way to a system of rulers and ruled.

Until recently it was generally believed that in the early Sumerian period the temple owned all the land of the city-state, but it has now been shown that the temple share amounted to perhaps no more than one-eighth of the whole. The rest of the land was originally owned by families or clans collectively, and could only be sold by agreement of all the prominent members of the family or clan. The buyers of such land would be members of what was coming to be the ruling class or nobility, and these people would thereby come to own land as private property in addition to what they held as family property. Such land would be worked by poor landless freemen. By such means there developed a social order in which there were three principal classes, that is, the nobility, the ordinary freemen, and the dependent freemen generally called 'clients'. A fourth class was constituted by slaves, who were mainly prisoners-of-war.

It has already been mentioned that the Sumerians were not the first inhabitants of what we now call Babylonia. Amongst their predecessors it is possible that one group was Semitic. If this was in fact so, this Semitic element would represent the first stage of a movement of peoples which has been going on throughout history. The use of the term 'Semitic' here requires explanation. The word has an unfortunate modern history because of its misuse by the Hitler régime, and for that reason many people are nervous of using it at all, except as a term covering certain languages. In the latter sense it denotes a closely knit group of languages which include, amongst modern tongues, Hebrew and Arabic, and, amongst ancient ones, Akkadian and Aramaic. However, *in the context of ancient history*, it is also perfectly legitimate to use the term 'Semites' in a racial sense, of a community of peoples having a single point of origin in prehistoric times. The ancient Semites (using the term as defined) were a people whose original home, as far as we know at present, was the interior of Arabia. From the end of the last Ice Age at about 8000 B.C. down to the present day Arabia (like much of the rest of the Near East) has suffered from relentless soil erosion, with the result that the desert area has extended and the population the land would support has become continually smaller. Throughout history the overflow from this population has been moving outwards to settle, usually in peaceful families, less commonly in larger warlike groups, on the more fertile fringes of the great desert.

One reason for guessing that there may have been Semites in South Iraq when the Sumerians first arrived is that some of the earliest Sumerian inscriptions contain words undoubtedly taken over from Semitic speech. Unfortunately, such evidence is not conclusive, because we do not know whether the period of contact between Sumerians and Semites which resulted in such borrowings was a matter of a few years or of centuries. The earliest certain movement of Semitic peoples into Iraq began in the second quarter of the third millennium (*i.e.* after 2750 B.C.), from which period there is evidence of a group, whom we know as the Akkadians, moving into northern Babylonia from the Jebel Sinjar area in East Syria.

The growing strength of the Semitic element in the population culminated in the coming into power of an Akkadian dynasty. In northern Babylonia the greatest Sumerian centre was the city of Kish, and the last King of Kish had as chief minister a man whom we know under the Semitic name of Sharrum-kin or Sargon, meaning 'true king', though this could hardly have been his original name. Sargon had founded a city called Agade (exact whereabouts still unknown), and when the King of Kish was over-thrown by a Sumerian ruler from farther south, Sargon took over the reins of government and gained control of the whole of the land later known as Babylonia (2371 B.C.). Sargon's descendants reigned for over a century, and we refer to this dynasty as the Dynasty of Agade, or, using the Semitic spelling of the name, the Dynasty of Akkad. (This is the ultimate origin of the term 'Akkadian' already used in several different contexts.)

Sargon ultimately extended his conquests up the Euphrates to North Syria, and possibly even into Asia Minor. He also conquered Elam to the east of Babylonia, and gained control of northern Iraq, the area later known as Assyria. In one of the cities of

Assyria there has been found a fine bronze mask which may have represented Sargon himself (*13*). Sargon's economic and political control of this unprecedentedly large area produced a marked rise in the standard of living of Babylonia, so that this period was remembered in tradition as a golden age.

The other great ruler of the Dynasty of Agade was the fourth, Sargon's grandson Naram-Sin. According to tradition, supported to some extent by archaeological evidence, Naram-Sin controlled an empire extending from Central Asia Minor to the southern end of the Persian Gulf. Ultimately the dynasty collapsed before the combined pressures of peoples from the northern and eastern mountains, despite the vigorous action taken by Naram-Sin(*11*).

11 Naram-Sin overcoming his enemies

The achievements of the Agade dynasty were of lasting importance despite its relatively short duration (2371–2230 B.C.). Especially significant was the introduction of new administrative methods, in particular the attempt at centralised government from a single city. This was destined to have far-reaching consequences for the future.

With the collapse of the central government of Agade, northern Babylonia was occupied by a mountain people called the Gutians, a savage race regarded with marked aversion in later tradition. However, the Gutians probably had little influence in southern Babylonia, which was still predominantly Sumerian both in race

12 Gudea, ruler of Lagash

and culture, and from this time the cities of this area once again rose to prominence. Under the Dynasty of Akkad, Agade had been the principal port of the country, but with this eliminated by the Gutian conquest, trade, and the wealth resulting from it, began to flow up the Persian Gulf into the southern cities. One of the cities which flourished at this time and about which we are particularly well informed is Lagash, under its ruler Gudea (12). This ruler's greatest achievement (from his own point of view) was the rebuilding of the temple of the city god, and he left a considerable number of inscriptions relating to this. These inscriptions give us valuable details about the international trade of the time. From them we learn that

Cedar beams from the Cedar-mountain [Lebanon]
He had landed on the quayside . . .;
Gudea had . . . bitumen and gypsum
Brought in . . . ships from the hills of Madga [Kirkuk?]. . . .
Gold dust was brought to the city-ruler from the Gold-land [Armenia]. . . .
Shining precious metal came to Gudea from abroad,
Bright carnelian came from Melukhkha [the Indus valley?].

Politically, however, the most important feature of the new period was the return to prominence of the city of Ur. Already at an earlier period (around 2600 B.C.) Ur had been a leading centre of Sumerian civilisation, and it was in royal tombs of that period that Sir Leonard Woolley discovered the famous art treasures with which his name is associated (14–16). Now, at about 2100 B.C., Ur

32

13 King Sargon of Agade (?)
Bronze mask from Kuyunjik, c. 2350 B.C.

14–16 Harp, gold helmet and dagger
From Ur, c. *2600* B.C.

became the capital of a Sumerian dynasty, known as the Third Dynasty of Ur, which governed the whole of Mesopotamia in an efficient bureaucracy. Wealth flowed into the capital by way of the Persian Gulf, and we have some of the actual trading documents, showing that the great temple of Ur exported textiles and oil to a distant port called Makkan, importing in exchange copper, beads and ivory.

This dynasty collapsed after about a century, leaving Babylonia in temporary chaos. The main factor in the collapse was a fresh movement of Semitic peoples, this time the group called the Amurru or Amorites.

17 Lady of the time of Gudea

Chapter II

KINGDOMS RISE AND FALL

A PEOPLE called the Amorites are well known to readers of the Old Testament, where the term is used for one of the main groups of inhabitants of Palestine before the final entry of the Hebrews under Joshua. These Biblical Amorites were descendants of settlers who had come in from the desert several centuries before. They had formed part of a great group of peoples, called in cuneiform sources the Amurrū (singular, Amurru), on the move in the Syrian desert and threatening all the fertile lands from Palestine to Iraq. 'Amurru' was probably originally the name of a particular tribe, but it came to be used of the whole of a certain wave of invaders from the Syrian desert.

The cuneiform sources give us our first hint of the movements of these Amurrū in an inscription from the Dynasty of Akkad. It comes from a document which refers to 'the year in which Sharka-lisharri [Naram-Sin's son and successor] defeated the Amurru in Basar', Basar being a mountain in the Syrian desert. References to these Amurrū become more frequent during the period of the Third Dynasty of Ur. One passage shows the contempt of the city-dwelling Sumerian for the savage desert dweller, who is described as 'the Amurru, . . . who eats raw meat, who has no house in his lifetime, and after he dies lies unburied'. Quickly, however, these Amurrū ceased to be despised desert savages and became a threat to the security, and finally to the very existence, of the Third Dynasty of Ur. Some of the rulers of that dynasty built fortifications against these people. Such measures did not, however, succeed in holding back the mounting pressure, and the ancient cities, first of the Middle Euphrates and then of Babylonia proper, gradually fell under the domination of these people.

The presence of people of the Amurrū group within the areas mentioned is shown in the first instance by the nature of the personal names, and afterwards, with the final collapse of the Third Dynasty of Ur, by the rise in a number of cities of dynasties in which the personal names, god names and institutions are obviously of Amorite origin. Such dynasties may for convenience be called 'Amorite', although some scholars regard the term as inaccurate when used in this sense. As might be expected in view of the geography, it is on the Middle Euphrates that a dynasty of Amorite origin is first in evidence, the city concerned being Mari. In other cities, some of the earlier peaceful Amorite settlers actually became officials in the service of the Third Dynasty of Ur. One such was a certain Ishbi-Erra, who was in charge of the city of Isin under the last King of Ur and who, after remaining loyal to the end, subsequently founded a dynasty of his own.

18 An early ruler of Mari

The Third Dynasty of Ur finally crumbled under the pressure of Amorite invaders, city after city ceasing to acknowledge the sovereignty of Ur. The final overthrow of the dynasty was, however, not actually the work of the Amorites, but of the Elamites (from southern Persia), who seized the opportunity to sack and occupy the capital, slaughtering the inhabitants and carrying away the King. This stunning blow, marking the final overthrow of the Sumerians as a political power, shows clear evidence in the relics of destruction found when the city was excavated. This disastrous event was long remembered in Babylonia.

With the breakdown of central control by Ur, dynasties arose in other cities, the two most prominent at first being Isin and Larsa. For this reason the century or so after the overthrow of Ur is often known as the Isin-Larsa period (2006–1894 B.C.). The Larsa dynasty gradually increased its influence at the expense of Isin, but was finally itself overthrown (1763 B.C.) by the sixth ruler of the Dynasty of Babylon, the great Hammurabi (1792–1750 B.C.).

The First Dynasty of Babylon (1894–1595 B.C.) is rightly thought

37

of, particularly during the reign of Hammurabi, as one of the highlights of ancient civilisation. It was an age of material prosperity, and it is also fortunately one of the periods about which we are best informed. There are not only many thousands of business documents and letters from Babylon and other cities, but we also have the collection of laws promulgated by Hammurabi himself(82). Together these documents make it clear that the pre-eminence of Hammurabi amongst his contemporaries, which enabled him to raise Babylon to a cultural supremacy which it was never to lose, was not due solely to his military ability. It also owed much to his political insight and aptitude for diplomacy, and to his administrative ability and concern for social justice throughout his land.

It would be a mistake to think of Babylon as the only city-state of significance at this period. Farther north there was the kingdom of Assyria, where another prince of Amorite origin, Shamshi-Adad I, an older contemporary of Hammurabi, established himself as king in 1814 B.C., and exerted considerable influence upon the regions to the south and south-west. In the early part of his reign Hammurabi had another powerful contemporary in the King of Eshnunna, who controlled the cities along the Diyala and in the neighbourhood of modern Baghdad. There were other Amorite centres of power in North Syria. The situation is summed up in a letter from this period which says

> There is no king who of himself alone is strongest. Ten or fifteen kings follow Hammurabi of Babylon, the same number follow Rim-Sin of Larsa, the same number follow Ibal-pi-El of Eshnunna, the same number follow Amut-pi-El of Qatanum [in Syria], and twenty kings follow Yarim-Lim of Yamkhad [in North Syria].

Another city-state of considerable importance until finally conquered by Hammurabi in 1761 B.C. was Mari, on the Middle Euphrates. It was a city of respectable antiquity, having been one of the outposts of Sumerian civilisation, and in the early second millennium B.C. was the capital of a kingdom extending over 200 miles along the river. In 1796 B.C. it experienced what must have been common in its history, a change of dynasty, when Shamshi-Adad of Assyria, benefiting by a palace revolution in Mari, placed his own son Yasmakh-Adad on the throne of Mari as his sub-king and representative. French archaeologists working before the war at Tell Hariri, the site of ancient Mari, had the good fortune to discover the royal archives from this period, and amongst them correspondence between Shamshi-Adad and the sub-kings who were his sons, as well as correspondence between the various rulers and their officials. Of less immediate human interest, but still very important for many details of life of the time, were the business documents. These various classes of texts, together with the physical remains of the buildings, combine to give us a surprisingly detailed picture of life at the time, of which some account is given in Chapter III.

The way of life which crystallised at this period under the shadow of Hammurabi was, with minor changes, the general pattern in Babylonia until, with the Persian conquest of the country in 539 B.C. and the subsequent growth of Hellenistic (Greek) influence, Babylonian civilisation finally withered away. The actual political achievements of Hammurabi, in bringing all Babylonia, and some regions beyond, under the control of the city of Babylon, did not long survive him. In the reign of Hammurabi's successor the people of the marsh country of South Babylonia broke away, forming a separate and long-lasting dynasty, whilst the same ruler came into conflict with the Cassites, a non-Semitic people from the mountains north-east of Babylonia.

After this first evidence of Cassite pressure, the following century saw a gradual increase both of peaceful immigration of individual Cassites, and of organised movements of armed bands. This may be connected with pressure upon the Cassites themselves by a southward movement of Indo-European and other peoples farther north. Amongst these peoples two of the most prominent groups were the Hittites and the Hurrians. The names of both groups will be recognised in the Bible (the Hurrians under the form Horites), but it should be borne in mind that the people called Hittites and Horites in the Bible may have had only a very slender and distant link with the groups known as Hittites and Hurrians in the cuneiform documents. The Hittites, an Indo-European people whose language was closely related to Latin, had begun to appear in northern Anatolia (eastern Turkey) early in the second millennium and had established a powerful kingdom in Central Anatolia soon after 1700 B.C. The Hurrians, who were neither Indo-European nor Semitic, had been centred on the region around Lake Van since before the Agade period, but had begun pushing southwards on a large scale by the early second millennium.

19 Ruins of a Cassite ziggurrat

These various pressures made the collapse of centralised government in Babylonia inevitable, though surprisingly the actual overthrow of the city of Babylon was at the hands of the most distant of the peoples mentioned, the Hittites from Central Anatolia. In 1595 B.C. the Hittite ruler made a sudden attack southwards into Syria, and then moved down the Euphrates to plunder Babylon. Political developments in his capital made the Hittite king return as suddenly as he had come, but Babylon was left powerless to resist a further aggressor, and Cassite forces descended from the hills to take over control of the capital and to impose their government upon North Babylonia. This Cassite dynasty, which rapidly adopted much of the culture and institutions of their predecessors in the land, lasted about 400 years (1595–c. 1150 B.C.)(19).

We return to the Hurrians, whom we have seen were moving southwards during the first half of the second millennium B.C. Associated with them at this time was an aristocracy of the race which we know as Indo-European or Aryan. The Aryans derived ultimately from the steppes of Russia, one of the original homes of the wild horse. Because of this, the Aryans were always found in association with the horse, and it was the Aryan migrants of the second millennium who introduced the horse-drawn chariot as an instrument of war(20). This chariot-owning Aryan aristocracy, ruling over a population which was largely Hurrian, had succeeded, shortly before 1500 B.C., in establishing a powerful kingdom centred upon the Habur area. We know this kingdom as Mitanni.

The kingdom of Mitanni is, oddly enough, best known not from evidence found in the kingdom itself, but from documents discovered in the land of the Hittites, in Syria, and above all in Egypt. All of these documents point to the considerable, if temporary, importance of Mitanni. The sources from Egypt are of two kinds. One is the Egyptian hieroglyphic documents, which have references to armed conflict with Mitanni in the Syrian region, the area in which the two States came into competition. The other Egyptian source, surprisingly, consists of clay tablets inscribed in cuneiform. These tablets are the famous El Amarna letters (*44*), found in Central Egypt at the end of last century, and constituting part of the diplomatic archives of the Egyptian kings at a period around 1400 B.C. These documents include letters to the Pharaoh from various princes of Palestine and Syria, from the kings of the Hittite land, Assyria and Babylonia, and from the King of Mitanni. The material concerned with the other rulers cannot be dealt with here, but the part of the correspondence involving Mitanni clearly shows that at the time Mitanni was on an equality with Egypt. These letters show that marriage alliances were made between Mitanni and Egypt, and give evidence of several instances in which Mitannian princesses were sent as brides for the King of Egypt. (It may be added that the Cassite ruler of Babylonia also made marriage alliances of this kind with Egypt.) Mitanni was so powerful at this period that its eastern neighbour Assyria was completely eclipsed and indeed at one time became actually a vassal of Mitanni. By 1350 B.C., however, Mitanni, torn by internal dynastic strife, had become so weak that it was virtually a dependency of the Hittite ruler Shuppiluliuma. Assyria was now able to reassert its independence, and this period, during the reign of Ashur-uballit I (1365–1330 B.C.), marks the

20 An Aryan horse-drawn chariot

beginning of the emergence of Assyria as one of the great Powers of the ancient Near East.

The Assyrians of the period 1350–612 B.C. were one of the most important, as well as one of the most maligned, peoples of the ancient world. Situated in northern Mesopotamia on the open plains immediately south of the great mountain ranges of Armenia, the people of Assyria had borne the brunt of the pressure generated by Indo-European peoples on the move in the steppes of Russia. We have already seen that Assyria was for a time actually a vassal of Mitanni, and in the following centuries, up to about 1000 B.C., it was to be subject to constant pressure from Aramaean peoples in the region to the west. The human response to this continual pressure was the development of a sturdy warlike people prepared to fight ruthlessly for their existence.

Assyrian political history from 1350 B.C. onwards shows a curious rhythm between periods of expansion and decline. First came a period of about a century in which Assyria secured itself from the threat of domination by Babylonia, and finally settled the Mitannian problem by turning what remained of that once powerful kingdom into the westernmost province of Assyria. It was during this period that Assyria first felt the pressure of a new wave of Aramaean peoples, called the Akhlamu, moving in from the west. At this time also, there arose in the mountains of Armenia a new tribal confederation, known as Uruatri or Urartu (the Biblical Ararat), shortly to become a kingdom of considerable importance.

This period of consolidation and expansion culminated in the capture by Tukulti-Ninurta I (1244–1208 B.C.) of Babylon. The significance of this was as if a King of Scotland in the Middle Ages had captured London. After this climax there was a sudden decline in the fortunes of Assyria. This was in part a direct consequence of the preceding period of expansion, in that repeated armed conflict with peoples to the north, east and south must have taken a serious toll of the cream of Assyrian manpower. Probably, however, a more important cause was the disturbed condition of the Near East as a whole. There was no longer a kingdom of Mitanni to wield political control in the Syrian area, whilst Egypt, which had frequently exercised suzerainty over Palestine and parts of Syria, was now quite unable to make its influence felt beyond its own boundaries. The Hittite Empire, which formerly had given political stability to Asia Minor and northern Syria, thereby protecting the trade routes, had, under the pressure of people migrating from Europe, rapidly crumbled away until by 1200 B.C. it was powerless. The disturbed situation throughout much of the Near East at this time, with the trade routes insecure and the villages depopulated, is reflected in the *Book of Judges*, for example in v 6-7: 'In the days of Shamgar, . . . caravans ceased and travellers kept to the byways. The peasantry ceased in Israel. . . .' This situation throughout the Near East was ultimately the result of a southward movement of peoples from Europe, of which the Greeks and probably the Biblical Philistines were a part. It was these people who ultimately broke up the Hittite Empire, destroyed Egyptian authority in Syria and Palestine, and seriously weakened Egypt itself by a direct attempt at invasion, which was beaten off by a great sea battle in about 1190 B.C. In these circumstances Assyrian trade with the Mediterranean region and Asia Minor was disastrously affected, so that Assyria may have been unable to obtain adequate supplies of such basic materials as metals, for which Asia Minor was one of the chief sources. For a short period Assyria fell under the suzerainty of Babylonia, which by reason of its geographical position was largely screened from the trouble caused by the situation in Asia Minor and Syria.

Babylonia, though more favourably placed than Assyria, did not altogether escape the effects of the general dislocation throughout the Near East, and it was during this period that the Cassite dynasty was finally overthrown. From the consequent chaos there emerged a new dynasty, known as the Second Dynasty of Isin, of which the most important ruler was Nebuchadnezzar I (1124-1103 B.C.). This King succeeded in extending Babylonian control over the mountain regions east and north-east of his country.

The establishment of stable conditions in Babylonia and the securing of the trade routes from farther east had a cumulative effect on the whole of Mesopotamia, and the end of the twelfth century marks the beginning of a new period of Assyrian expansion under Ashur-resh-ishi (1133-1116 B.C.) and his son Tiglath-Pileser I (1115-1077 B.C.). The former threw off the political suzerainty of Babylonia, and took the offensive both against the Akhlamu to the west and the mountain tribes to the east, thus giving security over a considerably greater area and the possibility of economic prosperity. Tiglath-Pileser had to deal with a direct threat resulting from the southward movement of peoples already referred to. This occurred when a large body of Mushku (the people known in the Old Testament as Meshech and in Greek literature as the Phrygians) moved into the Assyrian province of Kummukh in South Asia Minor. Tiglath-Pileser penetrated into Asia Minor to drive off these invaders, and thereby ensured Assyrian security in the north-west. With his northern flank secured, he was now able to conduct an expedition to the coast of Syria, where he received tribute: this was probably another way of saying that the Phoenician cities agreed to trade in timber and other commodities. Tiglath-Pileser also made diplomatic contact with the King of Egypt, from whom he received a live crocodile as a gesture of good will. The increased material prosperity resulting from Tiglath-Pileser's success in opening and maintaining the trade routes across western Asia is reflected in a considerable amount of building activity in connection with the temples of Assyria.

Soon after the death of Tiglath-Pileser the pendulum swung once again, so that a long period of difficulty and stress followed a time of relative prosperity. The main cause of the setback on this occasion was the growing pressure of the Aramaeans, already mentioned. This time Babylonia was affected as much as, or even more than, Assyria, so that ultimately an Aramaean prince, Adad-apal-iddinam (1067–1046 B.C.), was able to usurp the throne of Babylonia. The Assyrian ruler of the time, Ashur-bel-kala (1074–1057 B.C.) was not only unable to assist the legitimate Babylonian ruler, but was even driven to recognise the usurper and make a marriage alliance with him.

The pressure of the Aramaean racial movement had passed its peak by 1000 B.C., and during the following century Assyria made a slow recovery. This became marked during the reign of Adad-nirari II (911–891 B.C.). Under him Assyria effected a military expansion, and was able to safeguard its boundaries to south and east, and to protect the trade routes to the west by establishing fortified posts along the Middle Euphrates and in the Habur region. The security achieved by Adad-nirari II's policy is reflected in economic well-being, and in one inscription this King writes: 'I built administrative buildings throughout my land. I installed ploughs throughout the breadth of my land. I increased grain stores over those of former times. . . . I increased the number of horses broken to the yoke. . . .' River trade was of importance, and is reflected in the rebuilding of the quay wall of the capital Ashur on the Tigris. Agriculture flourished (21).

Adad-nirari II's successors (Tukulti-Ninurta II, 890–884 B.C.,

Ashurnasirpal II, 883–859 B.C., and Shalmaneser III, 858–824 B.C.) successfully continued the policy of military and economic expansion, gradually extending the area controlled by Assyria until the whole region from the Mediterranean coast to the Zagros Mountains, and from Cilicia to Babylonia was either directly administered by Assyria or ruled by vassals accepting Assyrian

21 Irrigation, the basis of Assyrian agriculture

overlordship. All the trade routes of the Near East, except those of Palestine, thus came into Assyrian hands.

It was during the reign of Shalmaneser III that Assyria first came into conflict with the kingdom of Israel, though the incident concerned is known only from the Assyrian records and not from the Bible. The clash occurred when the Syrian and Palestinian States formed a coalition to meet an Assyrian expedition to the Mediterranean in 853 B.C. According to the Assyrian records the coalition forces included '2,000 chariots and 10,000 soldiers of Akhabbu of the land of Sir'ala'. Akhabbu of Sir'ala was unquestionably Ahab of Israel. Shalmaneser claimed a defeat of the western forces, a claim borne out by the fact that a monument of four years later shows an emissary of Jehu, Ahab's successor, paying tribute (25).

Assyrian contact with Syria from this time is reflected in the collections of ancient Near Eastern art in modern museums. As we learn from the Bible (*1 Kings* x 18, xxii 39; *Amos* iii 15, vi 4), decoration in ivory was much appreciated in Palestine; and it seems that the Assyrian kings shared this taste. Syrian craftsmen were famous for their skill in ivory carving, and so from this time onwards the Assyrian kings carried off such men to the cities of Assyria, where they were employed in beautifying the royal palaces. Great quantities of carved ivory have been found at Nimrud, the site of the ancient capital Calah (22, 83).

Towards the end of the reign of Shalmaneser III (23) there was a rebellion involving some of the principal Assyrian cities. The great ancient cities of Assyria and Babylonia had always claimed a

22 Carved ivory from Nimrud

degree of independence, and in times of crisis the kings were often forced to recognise this by exempting the citizens from certain forms of taxation and liability to forced labour. It is likely that the long period of growing Assyrian power since the time of Adad-nirari II had put the King in a strong position, in which he was able to whittle away the privileges of the ancient cities of Assyria. This was probably one of the factors which led to the insurrection. It was finally put down, and Shalmaneser was succeeded by his accepted heir, Shamshi-Adad V (823–811 B.C.). This King continued the policy of his predecessors, undertaking military action in the north and north-east to defend Assyrian interests against Urartu and the Medes (an Iranian people who had recently migrated into North-West Persia). He also extended the area under his direct control to include the north-eastern edge of Babylonia, along the Diyala, and even intervened within Babylonia itself to impose submission upon some tribes called the Kaldu, whom we later know as Chaldaeans. These tribes, occupying the most southerly part of Babylonia, were virtually independent of the weak Babylonian King, and it may have been their interference with trade routes from the Persian Gulf region which led to Shamshi-Adad's action against them.

From about 800 B.C. Urartian influence began to expand, especially in the North Syrian area, at the expense of Assyria, and the following half century saw a drastic decline in the fortunes of Assyria. Conditions within the homeland became so bad that in 746 B.C. there was a revolt in the capital, Calah, the whole of the royal family being murdered.

The man who came to the throne, who was probably of royal descent though not of the family of his predecessor, was a certain Pul, who took as his throne name Tiglath-Pileser (27). Tiglath-Pileser III (745–727 B.C.) was one of the most able of Assyrian

46

23 Shalmaneser III
From Nimrud, c. *838* B.C.

24 Ashurnasirpal II
From Nimrud, c. *870* B.C.

25 Jehu's emissary paying tribute
From the black obelisk of Shalmaneser III at Nimrud

26 Ashurbanipal feasting with his wife
From Kuyunjik, seventh century B.C.

kings. He undertook extensive administrative reforms, reducing the power of provincial governors and at the same time increasing the efficiency of provincial administration (pp. 110–13). His reign saw a fresh extension of Assyrian influence to Babylon in the south and to Syria and Palestine in the west. His successor, Shalmaneser V (726–722 B.C.) maintained the same general policy; he is best known for his siege of Samaria, the

27 Tiglath-Pileser III

capital of Israel, which culminated, in accordance with the usual Assyrian policy, in the deportation to Assyria of the best of the population of the land (2 Kings xvii 6).

The story of the remaining period of the Assyrian Empire is one of continual expansion up to just after 640 B.C., and then a dramatic collapse. The principal kings of this period (known as the Sargonid period after the first of them) were Sargon II (721–705 B.C.), Sennacherib (704–681 B.C.), Esarhaddon (680–669 B.C.), and Ashurbanipal (680–626 B.C.). The political events of individual reigns need not detain us, but it may be useful to say a word about the men themselves. Sargon seems to have had a taste for poetry, and some of his annals are written in an elegant verse form as against the dry prose of some other Assyrian kings. (It is not of course suggested that Sargon personally composed the annals in verse.) Sennacherib is generally thought of as a ruthless barbarian, not perhaps without justification, for he was one of the few conquerors of Babylon to sack that centre of culture. At the same time he was, like many other barbarians, very interested in technological progress. His boast was that he had invented a new method of metal casting, devised new irrigation equipment, and found new mineral resources. He was also proud of having laid out Nineveh as his new capital, with parks to beautify it and a new

28 The Jerwan aqueduct

aqueduct(*28*) to give it a plentiful supply of good water. Of Esarhaddon little is known apart from his military and political achievements. In the political sphere he tried two new ideas, both of which had disastrous results. One was to attempt to incorporate Egypt into his Empire: this over-stretched Assyrian military resources and was one factor underlying the later collapse. The other new policy was to bequeath Babylonia to one son and Assyria and the rest of the Empire to another: the result here was that the two brothers, at first the best of friends, became personally involved in the old tensions between Assyria and Babylonia, so that civil war broke out. This, however, is to anticipate.

A word may be said here about the succession in Assyria. Although the kingship was normally treated as hereditary, it did not necessarily pass to the oldest son. Esarhaddon, for example, specifically emphasised that he was the chosen heir despite his being a younger son:

> Of my big brothers I was their little brother. At the command of Ashur . . . [and other gods], my father . . . formally promoted me in the assembly of my brothers, (saying) thus: 'This is the son of my succession.' When he asked (the gods) Shamash and Adad by liver-divination, they answered him a definite 'Yes!', (saying) thus: 'He is your successor.' He therefore paid respect to their solemn word and he assembled the people of Assyria, small and great, (with) my brothers the seed of my father's house, and he made them swear their solemn oath before Ashur . . . [and other gods], the gods of Assyria, the gods who dwell in heaven and earth, to protect my succession.

The accession of a king, if approved by the gods, was accompanied by various favourable signs. Esarhaddon said that when he ascended (after putting down an attempted usurpation), 'there blew the south wind, the breath of Ea, the wind whose blowing is good for the exercise of kingship; favourable signs appeared in the heavens and on the earth'.

The son to whom Esarhaddon bequeathed Assyria and the major part of the Empire was Ashurbanipal(26). This King prided himself on his literacy and tells us: 'I grasped the wisdom of Nabu [the scribal god], the whole of the scribal art of all the experts.' Some Assyriologists, with an elder-sisterly attitude to cuneiform studies, consider such a boast a presumption on the part of a mere Assyrian monarch, but we have no real evidence entitling us to dismiss Ashurbanipal's claim. Certainly he was keenly interested in cuneiform literature, for it was he who was mainly responsible for collecting one of the great libraries of Nineveh, the source of the thousands of Kuyunjik tablets (p. 26).

The civil war between Ashurbanipal and his brother in Babylon undoubtedly seriously weakened the Empire. None the less, when Ashurbanipal finally captured Babylon in 648 B.C., his position seemed superficially as strong as ever, so that between then and 639 B.C. he was able to undertake a series of campaigns to overrun Elam. There were, however, fresh factors in the world scene. In Iran, north of Elam, the Medes, a group of vigorous Iranian tribes (a branch of the Indo-European race) who had migrated into the area at about 900 B.C., were becoming a force to reckon with. Already at the time of Esarhaddon they had been of sufficient importance for that King to bind them by treaty to support his arrangement for the succession after his death, and by 650 B.C. they had consolidated themselves into a powerful kingdom which could, and ultimately did, successfully oppose Assyria. North of Assyria, the kingdom of Urartu had been knocked out by fresh hordes from Central Asia, who penetrated deep into Asia Minor. Although Ashurbanipal succeeded for a while in using them to his own advantage (as when he set them against a king on the coast of Asia Minor who was supporting the independence movement in Egypt), it was only a matter of time before some of these hordes turned against Assyria itself.

We know very little about Ashurbanipal's reign after 639 B.C. except that the situation for Assyria was becoming increasingly grave. When Ashurbanipal died in 626 B.C. a certain Nabopolassar, relying on support from the Chaldaean (Kaldu) tribes of Babylonia, assumed the kingship of that land, although Ashurbanipal's successors Ashur-etillu-ili and Sin-shar-ishkun seem to have retained partial authority in parts of the southern kingdom.

However, Nabopolassar made an alliance with the Medes, and his complete success against Assyria was almost inevitable.

At the very end Assyria found an unexpected ally in Egypt, a Power which would not view favourably the eventual handing over of the trade routes of the Near East, hitherto controlled by Assyria, to the mercy of such upstart and unpredictable people as the Medes and Chaldaeans. The Egyptian support was, however, too late to restore the old order and Nineveh fell in 612 B.C., the remnant of the Assyrian forces, with their Egyptian allies, making a last stand at Carchemish in 605 B.C., only to meet with final defeat. The Assyrian Power was irrevocably at an end.

Nabopolassar died at this moment. His son and successor Nebuchadnezzar II had been his father's Commander-in-Chief, and was a general of great experience and ability. He grasped the remains of the Assyrian Empire, and extended his authority to the Egyptian border, his two attacks upon Jerusalem (597 and 587 B.C.), and the deportation of the Jews to Babylonia, being very well known. These were, in fact, simply incidents in Nebuchadnezzar's struggle to impose his authority over an area which the new Egyptian dynasty was coming to regard as its own sphere of influence. The Medes at the same time extended their realm to include the old kingdom of Urartu and much of Asia Minor.

The Neo-Babylonian Empire, as the empire founded by Nebuchadnezzar is usually called, suffered economically from the fact that the Medes now controlled the trade routes from farther east passing through the old kingdom of Urartu and Asia Minor to the west. It was in an attempt to rectify this that the Neo-Babylonian rulers tried to extend their authority in the south-west, so that they would benefit by the trade routes coming up from Arabia. We have seen that Nebuchadnezzar took steps to control the whole of Syria and Palestine, and later in his reign there is evidence that he unsuccessfully attempted an invasion of Egypt itself. His second successor, Neriglissar, was probably actuated by similar economic motives when he undertook a campaign into Asia Minor (just before 556 B.C.). It was, however, the last Neo-Babylonian King, Nabu-naʾid (Nabonidus) (555–539 B.C.), who made the most determined endeavours to put the Empire on a sounder economic footing. Much of his reign was spent in western Arabia, where he established a chain of military colonies along what is known as the 'incense route' from Teima to Yathrib (modern Medina).

By the time of Nabu-naʾid relations between Babylonia and the

29 Map of the Assyrian Empire

Medes had gravely deteriorated, and Nabu-naʾid in the early years of his reign had looked with favour upon a certain prince who was in revolt against the Median King. This prince was Cyrus the Persian. Cyrus, however, once he had gained control of the Median Empire, proceeded upon an expansionist policy which quickly brought him into conflict with Babylonia. By brilliant generalship he succeeded in gaining control, in 547 B.C., of the whole of Asia Minor as far as the Greek settlements on the west coast, and then seized the eastern part of Assyria, which of course fell within the Babylonian sphere of influence. War broke out, and Cyrus invaded the Babylonian Empire over a wide front. Public opinion throughout the civilised world at this time is reflected in *Isaiah* xlv 1 and 4, where the Hebrew prophet hails Cyrus as the chosen one of the Lord. Nabu-naʾid was much less happily placed. Even within Babylonia he was unpopular, in part from the economic difficulties which faced the country and in part from attempts he had made at religious reform, and when Cyrus finally marched upon Babylon, he already had many adherents within the city. Babylon fell to him in 539 B.C.

The Persian Empire, into which Egypt was incorporated in 525 B.C., now exceeded in extent any which had gone before it, and of this Empire Babylonia and Assyria formed only one province. Babylonian and Assyrian culture had, however, a continuing influence, and amongst other things Persian art (*30*), civil administration and military science owed much to their Babylonian or Assyrian roots. Babylon was, if not the political, certainly the administrative and cultural capital of the whole Persian Empire.

After 500 B.C. the Persian Empire came into collision with Greece, and conflict continued intermittently until in 331 B.C. the

30 Persian bronze and silver bracelets

Macedonian Alexander the Great overthrew the Persian power at a battle near Arbela, proceeding afterwards to extend his authority to the borders of India. Had Alexander lived, it was his intention to establish a world empire with its capital at Babylon, but his premature death at Babylon in 323 B.C., at the age of thirty-two, left his territories to be divided up amongst his generals. The eastern provinces, including Babylonia and Assyria, eventually fell to Seleucus I (301–281 B.C.). Under the Seleucids Babylonia and Assyria came increasingly under Hellenistic cultural influence, and Akkadian, which had already been superseded by Aramaic as the language of everyday speech, was no longer even written, except for religious or astronomical purposes. The old culture of Babylonia and Assyria was dead, and the future lay with Palestine, Greece, and Rome.

Chapter III

LIFE AT AN AMORITE COURT

A T the end of 1933 French archaeologists began excavations at a site called Tell Hariri on the Middle Euphrates in eastern Syria, continuing there until the end of 1938 and resuming again after the war. The site was quickly proved to be that of the ancient city of Mari, already known from cuneiform documents from other places as the seat of an important dynasty. Large numbers of cuneiform tablets were found, the most important single find being that of an archive of about 13,000 tablets in 1936. Another remarkable discovery was the remains of a huge palace which, when excavated, proved to contain nearly 300 rooms and to cover some six acres, that is, as much as sixty or seventy good-class suburban houses with their gardens. The state of preservation of the walls was surprisingly good for a building 4000 years old, remaining in parts to a height of up to sixteen feet, with some of the doorways intact. The archaeologist in charge of the excavations was even able to write to the effect that many of the domestic installations of the palace, such as the kitchens, baths and pantries, could still have functioned almost without any repairs(31). On some of the plastered walls there were still to be seen the original mural paintings(32).

It is now clear that the palace was pillaged in the early second millennium (in fact by Hammurabi of Babylon, in about 1760 B.C.), and the cuneiform documents shed a flood of light on the life of the time. They give us information not only on the international scene just before the sack of the city, but also on the history of the occupants of the palace, providing us with a picture, often in considerable detail, of the private and public circumstances in which they lived.

31 Terracotta bath from Mari

32 Mural painting at Mari

One must imagine the city as lying within a strong defensive wall. From a distance the most conspicuous building, as in the majority of Mesopotamian cities, was the ziggurrat or great temple-tower, standing perhaps 150 feet above the plain, with a number of temples grouped at its foot. Not far off was the huge expanse of the great palace already referred to. This palace was of course not merely a royal residence, but was also an administrative centre from which all the work of what we should call the Civil Service and Foreign Service was directed. It is this that accounts for the presence within the palace of Mari of the thousands of letters and administrative and judicial documents. In contemporary English terms the royal palace of this period is to be thought of as Whitehall rather than Buckingham Palace. Even this does not cover all the functions of the palace of Mari. Part of it was a business centre, with warehouses where merchants could deposit their goods, and another section must have served as barracks for at least a part of the contingent of troops stationed permanently within Mari. Mari was also a military depot, and it was probably within the palace courtyards that equipment such as battering-rams and siege-towers were stored until required elsewhere.

57

Palaces fulfilling functions similar to those of the palace of Mari existed, though on a smaller scale, in the other principal towns of the kingdom.

Naturally, part of the palace of Mari constituted the private quarters and the State apartments of the King himself. At the time we are imagining, this was Yasmakh-Adad, a younger son of Shamshi-Adad of Assyria. To judge by the correspondence which passed between him and his elder brother and his stern old father, Yasmakh-Adad seems to have been regarded as somewhat frivolous and lacking in a sense of responsibility. We certainly find him getting into a number of scrapes for bungling his official duties, but, as we shall see, there was so much for which he was responsible that an occasional slip-up was excusable. Despite any failings which his father and elder brother may have seen in him, there were strong ties of affection between the members of the family. Thus we find, in one letter, Shamshi-Adad strongly insisting that Yasmakh-Adad should come to his city for a fortnight's stay, whilst on many an occasion Yasmakh-Adad's older brother went out of his way to get him out of trouble.

There are hints in the letters passing between Yasmakh-Adad and his father and brother that he was fond of good company. If indeed this was so, Yasmakh-Adad had plenty of opportunity for indulging in his taste, as at any time the number of people in residence at his Court might run into hundreds. These included members of his own family, visiting ambassadors, permanent palace officials, ministers and administrators, officers of the garrison, and high officials from other towns temporarily in Mari. There were also ladies of various classes from wives to religious prostitutes, but these probably had their own quarters and did not mix with the men in the general business of the day.

Not much is known about the actual routine of the palace at this period. It seems clear that the King held a Court each morning, at which such officials and ambassadors as had business to transact would be present. Here the King would have read to him by his ministers letters sent from his father or brother or from foreign rulers or private persons. Probably many of the letters were read out publicly, though others were, from their contents, obviously for the King's ear alone. Sometimes a correspondent might provide his ambassador with a dummy letter full of trivialities to be read in public, leaving the ambassador to give the King's chief minister the genuine communication in a private interview on a suitable occasion. Another of the King's functions at his public audience would be the settlement of legal disputes. Serious lawsuits, which officials had considered too grave or too difficult for them to settle, would on these occasions be referred to the King for a decision.

Part of a typical royal day must have been taken up with religious ceremonies, since in ancient Mesopotamia the King always played an essential part in the State religion. Indeed, at some periods the King was actually considered divine, though not at this time. In the course of his religious duties the King might be required to visit one or other of the temples of Mari, or even of other towns in the kingdom, to officiate at rituals or to perform certain ceremonies. This could involve such things as slaughtering sheep for sacrifice, making reports to the gods on State affairs, receiving investiture from the gods, or simply paying respects to the images of the gods (46). (In speaking of gods, we include here goddesses.) The King would certainly also have to attend certain feasts of the gods, and possibly some of their daily meals. The use of the terms 'feasts' and 'meals' here is not to be taken as metaphorical: they were real meals with real food in large quantities set out on tables

33 A religious ceremony at Mari

59

before the images of the gods. Who really ate the food we can only guess, but no doubt the priests and their families lived well.

At a later period the gods had four meals a day, two main meals and two snacks, and it is a reasonable assumption that they already did so at the period we are considering. As to what the humans in the palace did, we are not certain in this respect, but we do know that one of the daily meals was a formal dinner. The King partook of this in the company of visiting dignitaries and some of his own officials, and the number dining at the King's table might be anything from a dozen to a hundred. Whether the ladies of the Court were admitted to this is not altogether certain, but it seems likely that they took their meals separately. This is suggested by a ration list in which provisions are specified for 'the religious prostitutes, the harem women, the lady singers'.

At the dinner distinguished guests wore a special robe given them by their royal host. This was what in current jargon we might call a 'status symbol', and there was heart-burning amongst those at Court who did not receive this honour. At present our information about what the guests ate at the royal dinner is distinctly one-sided. Lists of provisions for the royal meals have been found in the palace, and as they contain no meat courses, one might rashly conclude that the Court was vegetarian. In fact, however, we know that beef and mutton were eaten by people who could afford them, and probably the reason we have no mention of meat is that there was a separate butcher's department in the palace with its own accounts, which are still awaiting discovery. Fish was also eaten, some species being particularly sought after. Amongst other foodstuffs we hear about, four varieties of 'bread' are distinguished, of which the commonest was an unleavened bread in the form of thin crisp disks made from whole-meal barley flour. Another type was specifically described as 'leavened bread', whilst the others were

34 A goddess from Mari

probably what we should refer to as pastries, since they contained such ingredients as sesame oil and something called 'honey'. The doubt about the latter term is that the same Akkadian word sometimes means honey from wild bees and sometimes date-syrup. Amongst vegetables in common use at this time were cucumbers, peas, beans, plants rather like cress, and garlic. There was a kind of truffle which was

35 A cellar

considered a great delicacy, and we have mention of baskets of them being sent to the King. The commonest fruit was, of course, the date, but grapes and figs are also commonly mentioned.

As to beverages, both beer and wine were available(35). The beer was produced locally, though wine had to be imported from the kingdoms to the north and north-east. In some of these kingdoms the rulers were very proud of their vintages.

On special occasions there would be a Court entertainment, of which no doubt a prominent feature would be music and over-indulgence in liquor. The music was provided by specially trained slave-girls. It is also likely that poets or minstrels recited traditional stories, of an improving or amusing nature, such as fables in which the date-palm and tamarisk, or the fox and dog, argued their respective merits. Several compositions which were probably put to this purpose have come down to us.

It is now time to turn from Yasmakh-Adad's relaxations to the serious business of his life.* His personal responsibility was considerable, covering a remarkably wide range of matters. Officials and private people would constantly be sending problems for the King to solve. A ship might have been wrecked on the Euphrates,

*All the following examples of royal responsibility are taken from documents of the period under discussion, but a few of them actually occur in relation to rulers other than Yasmakh-Adad.

so that the grain it was carrying for the palace had had to be beached. What was to be done about the grain and the crew? An ox intended for the palace had grown so fat and heavy that it could not stand, still less be driven to Mari. The official shouldered off the problem on to the King: 'Let my lord send instructions about this matter.' Another man wrote to say that the chariot with which the King had provided him had broken down in the course of his journeys: could the writer please have a replacement. The King was informed that the wall of some town was falling down and there was no mason available to deal with it: could he please send either a mason to repair the wall or a doctor in case of accident. A lion had been caught, and, although no instructions had been received from the King, it was now on its way to the capital by ship, for fear it escaped. A palace official had died and left an orphan son without means of support: would the King be kind enough to make arrangements. A wife had either run away or been kidnapped and gone to another country: would the king please intercede with the foreign ruler for her return.

Other problems the King might receive to deal with were of a religious nature. Thus one official sends a message from the State god Dagan, who is seen on more than one occasion to have become rather impatient at neglect: 'Dagan has sent me a message, "Send to your lord, and in the coming month, on the fourteenth, let the *pagrai* sacrifice be performed." ' The King was also constantly having to take account of omens reaching him. Religious functionaries were an important part of the personnel of any city or district, and amongst such people diviners (that is, priests who professed to foretell the future in matters affecting the State) were considered almost indispensable. Indeed, in one letter Yasmakh-Adad's brother points out to him that 'there can be no *patum* [a particular administrative district] without a diviner'. The actual procedure in divination was most commonly to dedicate and sacrifice a sheep and then examine its liver and lungs. The theory was that the gods would write their intentions on the sheep's organs by signs which could be interpreted by the learned (36). Omens so obtained were duly reported to the King and apparently taken seriously. A correspondent reports:

In the city of Sagaratim, at the monthly sacrifice and my lord's sacrifice, I examined the omens. The left side of the 'finger' [a projecting piece of the organ] was split, the middle 'finger' of the lungs was over to the left. It is a sign of fame. Let my lord be happy.

Omens had to be taken before a ruler or high official went on a journey, and there were also diviners on service with the army. Even the tactics of military units might be decided by the manner in which the diviners interpreted the omens. We have a letter specifically saying, in connection with arrangements for the disposition of troops, 'The diviners shall

36 Clay model of a sheep's internal organ

weigh up the omens, and according to the appearance of favourable omens 150 men shall go out or 150 men shall come in.' However, despite the importance attached to omens, kings were sometimes intelligent enough, or (from the point of view of the diviners) pig-headed enough, to disregard them and rely on their own judgement. We see this possibility recognised by an official who, in reporting the omens, told the King that they were not favourable for a certain military expedition and begged the King to pay serious heed to them. None the less, he accepted the fact that the King might please himself, and expressed himself willing to do his part whatever course was decided upon. Such independence of thought was however discouraged, and there existed cautionary tales in the form of legends about the unpleasant fate which befell kings of old, such as Naram-Sin of Agade, who had been foolish enough to act against the omens.

One of the biggest preoccupations of the King must have been his control of his officers and what we might call his Civil Service. It was necessary to have officials to administer the various towns and districts, to see to the collection of taxes (mostly in kind), to control irrigation, and to maintain order; and officers were also needed for the army. In the absence of currency issued by the State, there was no convenient way of providing for such officials except by the grant of land. Thus the King of Mari had to arrange for this. The way in which this distribution of estates was done was often a cause of complaint, and we frequently find kings appealed to by those who felt they had been hard-treated in this respect. A typical complaint from a disgruntled officer runs: 'Neither corn nor field has been appointed to me. . . . I cannot cultivate a field, I cannot eat rations with the soldiers of the fortress. I am starving. Let my lord appoint (something) for me.'

It was technically the King's task to appoint governors over the cities, but in practice the citizens could make their own nominations, which might well be accepted, especially if accompanied with a substantial present. We find this situation in the following letter:

> To my lord Yasmakh-Adad say, thus says Tarim-Shakim [a high-ranking civil servant]: 'Baqqum, the Man [*i.e.* ruler] of the city Tizrakh, has gone to his fate [*i.e.* died]. Now the citizens of Tizrakh have come and they say "Set Kali-Il (to serve) as Agent (over) us." Furthermore, he has delivered one mina of silver to the Palace (in consideration of) this being decreed. Now, therefore, I have dispatched Kali-Il before my lord. Let my lord set him to the sheikhdom of Tizrakh, and let him accept from him the one mina of silver as appropriate.'

Another of the many formal responsibilities of the King was the regulation of the calendar. Throughout Mesopotamian history the calendar used was based on a year consisting of twelve lunar months. Since the average period from one new moon to the next is twenty-nine and a half days, twelve lunar months amount to 354 days, which is eleven and a quarter days short of a solar year. Thus after three years the lunar calendar would be thirty-three and three-quarter days out from the solar year, and would need an extra month put in (or 'intercalated') to bring it more or less into line. It was the King's duty to arrange for this, though of course he did not work it out personally but was advised by his astronomers.

Probably the heaviest part of the King's duties concerned his relations with foreign rulers, with problems ranging from runaway wives to war. There were always foreign ambassadors at Yasmakh-Adad's Court, and he himself had ambassadors at the Courts of other rulers. Some such officials might be more or less permanently attached to a particular Court, whilst others would be special envoys entrusted with negotiations about particular matters, and passing from one Court to another as circumstances required. Naturally we have no record of the business transacted verbally between ambassadors and the King, and our sources are solely the written documents brought by the envoys.

Relations between friendly rulers mostly concerned either trade or military aid. Kings gave each other military assistance not only by direct alliance but also, in small-scale operations, by the loan of troops. Such loans would be intended only for a limited action during a particular emergency, and since in such cases the lender and borrower are inclined to differ as to when the emergency is over, this frequently led to friction. We thus find complaints of the following kind from a ruler who had lent troops in this way: 'Since the god has destroyed the enemy and the days of cold weather have arrived, why are you retaining the servants of your brother?' Clearly the winter was regarded as a close season for military operations.

Kings of this period often sent each other presents, sometimes as genuine gifts designed to establish or retain friendly relations. Thus we find the King of Carchemish sending the King of Mari a present of wine. It was the King of Carchemish who was so proud of his wine, and on another occasion we find him writing: 'If there is no good wine . . . for you to drink, send me a message, and I will send you good wine.' At other times the sending of presents was a disguised form of trade, since a corresponding present was expected in return. If one of the kings was a mean man this was liable to lead to disappointment. Thus we find one disgruntled ruler, the petty King of the Syrian State of Qatna, who on one occasion thought he had made a bad bargain, and wrote to Ishme-Dagan, the brother of Yasmakh-Adad, to this effect:

> This thing is unspeakable! But yet I must speak it so that I may relieve my heart [almost 'so that I may get it off my chest']. You desired from me, as your request, two horses, and I had them sent to you. Now you have had twenty minas of lead brought to me. . . . The price of a horse here with us . . . is 600 (shekels) of silver [i.e. ten minas of silver]. But you have had only twenty minas of lead brought to me.

Since the price of lead was only one-fourteenth that of silver, there was some substance in the King of Qatna's complaint.

The merchants were important members of the community, and a king of this period would sometimes have to take up their case with a foreign ruler to protect their interests. Thus we find Yasmakh-Adad writing to the great Hammurabi of Babylon over a difficulty which had befallen one of the trading caravans from Mari. He writes:

> To Hammurabi say, thus says Yasmakh-Adad. 'Previously your brother [*i.e.* the writer of the letter, Yasmakh-Adad himself] dispatched a caravan to the city of Tilmun. [Tilmun was well to the south of Babylonia, so such a caravan would have to pass through Hammurabi's territory.] In due course this caravan returned. It was held up by Ili-Ebukh [some official of Hammurabi] in (connection with) a claim over a well. . . . They brought that caravan to Babylon safely before you. . . .'

Yasmakh-Adad then goes on to say what he would like done about the caravan.

Farmers as well as merchants might need the attention of the King to their affairs. In a land like his with a marginal rainfall, pasturage in particular areas often failed and the King would have to make arrangements for pasturing the large flocks of sheep belonging to him or to the various towns or temples. Sometimes, when conditions were particularly bad, this might involve coming to an arrangement with a neighbouring ruler to allow the flocks to cross into better-provided territory. Even direct military action would sometimes be linked up with agriculture, since there were times when measures had to be taken to prevent raids upon the cultivated areas by nomadic peoples from the desert.

The security of the land as a whole was in the last resort the responsibility of the King, and it almost goes without saying that all the purely military affairs of his State were under his direct supervision. The King's responsibilities in this sphere of course involved measures against possible enemies from outside, as well as the maintenance of civil order within the State. For these purposes there existed a standing army of about 10,000 arranged in basic units of 200 men. A large proportion of this standing army, about 4000 men, was usually garrisoned in the capital. In case of major trouble the standing army could be augmented by the levying of troops either from the citizens of the towns or from tribesmen. As is often the case, conscription of this kind was not always very popular, and various vigorous means of persuasion sometimes had to be used. We find one of the more drastic methods suggested by an official writing to the King, on an occasion when the men of a certain area had been called up for military service but were very slow in putting in an appearance. The officer in charge of the matter wrote: 'If the King approves, let them kill one of the guilty men, and cut off his head, and let them take it round amongst those towns. . . , so that the people may be afraid and will quickly assemble.' However, conscripts were not always so reluctant. In another letter an official, reporting that two groups of conscripts had arrived, said that they had no sickness amongst them and nothing wrong at all. In fact, as the official put it: 'In this campaign . . . there were no worries or anything of that sort, only laughing and singing as though they were at home. Their morale is good.'

All kinds of details would come to the King about his armed forces, not only reports of broader issues such as actual engagements with the enemy, but even such items as the attempted murder of one officer by another. He would also of course receive intelligence reports about troop movements in neighbouring States, of which the following is an example:

> To my lord Yasmakh-Adad say, thus says Warad-Sin. 'In the month of Tamkhiri, on the twenty-first day, in the evening, they brought a report from the town Yandikha in these terms, "The troops of the Man [*i.e.* ruler] of Eshnunna are grouping in force in the town Mankisu." '

Though a serious matter, such a report would by no means imply that war was inevitable, since difficulties between States were more often than not smoothed over by diplomatic exchanges. The most frequent use of the army was not in war between States, but in actions to deal with raids by the semi-nomadic tribesmen who still roamed the desert around the fringes of the settled lands. As a protection against such raids garrisons were posted at points along the border and in strategically sited towns. To raise a general alarm in the event of a serious attack at any point there was a special system. This involved a series of fire-beacons spaced across the country, whereby in emergency a warning could be rapidly flashed to the capital from the danger-point.

So far we have considered only that part of the life of Mari which was primarily related to the King. It may be useful to supplement the picture by what we know of other aspects of the life of the time.

We have very little evidence about the total population of Mari, but it is unlikely to have been more than 100,000 and may have been substantially less. It is well known that in Babylon at this time there was a fairly clear-cut division of the population into three classes, the *awilum* or full citizen, the *mushkenum* or second-class citizen, and the slave, who was not a citizen at all but a chattel. How far this system was reflected in Mari is uncertain. There were certainly slaves in Mari, and there were certainly noble families which seem to have occupied a privileged position, but on the whole the division between full and second-class citizens seems to have been less evident than at Babylon. The population certainly included people ranging from members of ancient families who had been in Mari since Sumerian times to recent immigrants from the desert, but whether such differences in origin were in general reflected in differences of status we do not know.

The State of Mari as a whole had a predominantly agricultural basis, but there were certain industries carried on in the towns, particularly at the capital itself, where there was considerable specialisation. Amongst other things, the capital was noted for the superior quality of the chariots made there. Census lists and other documents refer to people by their trades, and we find men described as boatman, carpenter, leather-worker, fisherman, potter or mason. Amongst other professions and trades known at this time are those of metal-workers, weavers, fullers, gem-cutters, jewellers, painters, and perfume-makers. An analysis of the lists mentioned indicates that about one-fifth of the population consisted of craftsmen, the remainder (apart of course from officials) being labourers. Not only grown men and women but also children of both sexes had to take their part in the work of the nation.

Workers were sometimes paid wholly in the form of rations of corn, wool, clothing, wine or oil, that is, their actual primary necessities. Alternatively they might be paid wholly or partly in silver, though not of course in coins, which were not invented until 1000 years later. Where payment was in kind, the actual amounts of the daily rations of the various commodities can sometimes be calculated. Thus we find, for example, '1 *gur* 15 *qa* for two men who for forty-three days dwelt in the house of the perfume-maker', which works out at about two-and-a-half pints of oil each a day. If this seems excessive, it should be remembered that this took the place both of edible fats and butter in the diet, and of soap and hair-cream amongst toilet accessories.

One of the industries carried on at Mari was tool production, and the city must have had a good name for this as raw materials were sent there from other places to be worked up. These tools were made of copper or bronze. Other objects made from these metals at this time included, to mention only a few things, swords, ploughshares, parts of chariots, pots and pans (though only as luxury goods for wealthy people), bangles, fish-hooks, needles, mirrors, braziers, tweezers, and knives. The precious metals gold and silver had long been known, but were too soft for anything except ornaments or valuable vessels, which were usually destined for the temples or the King. Gold at this time was worth four times as much as silver. Another metal used at the time, and for which Mari served as a centre of distribution, was known in Akkadian as *anakum*, which was either tin or lead. Iron is occasionally mentioned, and has even been found in excavations, but in only very small quantities, and was possibly used as jewellery, or more probably as amulets with magical properties. The technological advances which made possible the large-scale production of good quality iron had not yet been achieved. The rarity of iron is confirmed by the fact that a text of this period shows that the value of the metal was still twice that of gold.

One important industry within the kingdom of Mari had its main centre away from the capital. This was the production of bitumen, from the famous bitumen lake near Hit, at the southern end of the kingdom. The substance was produced in a liquid and a solid form, corresponding roughly to tar and pitch. It was important as a building material throughout the whole of Babylonia, being used as a damp course, as a mortar, and (mixed with ground limestone or similar materials) for surfacing floors or pavements.

Outside the towns, the great majority of the population was engaged in some form of farming, either the cultivation of the soil or the rearing of flocks of sheep or goats. Along the Middle Euphrates the cultivation of most crops is impossible without irrigation, and the irrigation system was perhaps the most vital part of the economy of the kingdom of Mari. This was well recognised, and we find a governor specifically pointing out to his King that 'if the waters are interrupted, the land of my lord will starve'. The same official even felt free to refuse the King's summons to the capital, on the plea that he was needed to supervise irrigation works.

Indications are that the irrigated area extended to a depth of three or four miles along the right (south) bank of the Euphrates for most of the two hundred or so miles of the kingdom of Mari. There was a whole network of canals, with special officials to supervise them, and in time of necessity all the able-bodied men of a district, townsmen as well as villagers, could be called out to work on them, either to clear them of rushes and water-weeds or to dig out sections where silt had accumulated or to build up and consolidate the banks against floods.

The staple crops of the kingdom were barley and sesame (p. 128). The details of agricultural operations depended upon the type of land, particularly upon whether it was virgin soil or an established field, but in general work began in July or August and involved two or three main stages. The first was deep ploughing, if this was considered necessary. Then came some form of harrowing or other process (such as rolling or hoeing) to break up the surface clods; more than one of these operations might be necessary. Finally, by December at the latest, came the sowing. This was done by means of a seeder plough, a special implement with a funnel which permitted the seed to be dropped directly into the furrow as it was cut (37).

The rainfall in the Mari area is just under six inches a year, falling mostly between December and February. This would be sufficient to make the seed germinate, but irrigation was essential to keep the crop growing. The barley would be ready for harvesting in May, when all available labour, including children, would be called out to deal with it.

The ploughs mentioned above were at this period drawn by oxen, which were more important as draught animals than as food, though they were eaten. It was oxen (not, as used to be thought, asses) which drew the carts present in the famous Royal Tombs of Ur (c. 2600 B.C.). Cows were milked, though they were of less importance in this respect than goats.

The other principal beast of burden at this time was the ass, which usually carried its load as a pack, though it might be used to draw a cart or as a riding beast. The horse, though it had by this time been introduced to the Near East from farther north, was still something of a novelty, and old-fashioned people considered it not quite the thing for a king to be seen riding one.

The animal of highest economic importance in the kingdom of Mari (and indeed

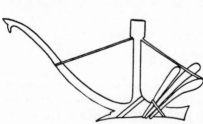

37 A seeder plough; Assyrian, first millennium B.C.

throughout Babylonia) was, however, the sheep, closely followed by the goat. These, provided their shepherds could save them from being driven off by nomadic raiders, could, then as now, usually pick up a living from patches of vegetation scattered about the desert, though when these failed, as they sometimes did,

38 Heavy Sumerian ass-drawn chariot

special Government arrangements might have to be made for grazing grounds elsewhere or the provision of fodder. Sheep and goats together provided the main source of meat, as well as the raw material for clothing and textiles. It is also a reasonable assumption, judging by the situation elsewhere in the Near East, that their milk was an important source of food, though there seems to be no specific evidence for this from Mari.

Chapter IV

THE SCRIBE IN BABYLONIAN SOCIETY

WITHOUT doubt, the most important man in the ancient society of Mesopotamia was the scribe. Kings might extend their sway over hitherto unknown regions, merchants might organise the importation of rare commodities from distant lands, the irrigation officials might set the labourers to utilise the bountiful waters of the rivers and to bring fertility to the soil, but without the scribe to record and transmit, to pass on the detailed orders of the administrators, to provide the astronomical data for controlling the calendar, to calculate the labour force necessary for digging a canal or the supplies required by an army, the co-ordination and continuity of all these activities could never have been achieved. Ancient Mesopotamian civilisation was above all a literate civilisation.

Writing began, so far as we know at present, in Sumer (southernmost Mesopotamia) at about 3000 B.C., the earliest examples we possess consisting of pictures drawn on lumps of clay(43). These earliest examples of writing already show, in the view of some experts, a certain development from what must have been the original form of the pictures, and there is the possibility that there may have been an even earlier stage of writing, of which we have no direct trace. This could have been used either in Sumer itself on some material, such as palm leaves, which has perished, or in the still unidentified earlier home of the Sumerians.

We cannot yet read the earliest writing discovered, and so cannot be sure beyond doubt what language it was intended to represent. The archaeological evidence gives, however, good reason to suppose that it was a form of the language we call Sumerian.

Despite the difficulties involved in dealing with a dead language apparently unconnected with any other known tongue, considerable advances have been made in the understanding of Sumerian during the past forty years. It was a language of the type which we call 'agglutinative' (meaning 'gluing together'), that is, instead of inflecting its roots like most of the languages we are familiar with, it kept all its roots unchanged and glued bits on to alter the sense. The earliest writing simply used pictures to represent whatever was to be noted down. This was quite straightforward as long as a storekeeper simply wanted to make a note such as 'five pigs', which might be represented as something like

but to draw pictures of verbs would generally be more difficult. The Sumerian inventors of writing often got over the difficulty by drawing some concrete object to suggest the idea of the verb. Thus, since a leg is used for either walking or standing, the picture of a leg could be used for the verbs 'to walk' and 'to stand'.

The picture of a head, with the mouth emphasised and a piece of bread alongside it, clearly represented the idea 'to eat'. A bird sitting on an egg was one way of indicating the idea 'to give birth'.

A class of words that a scribe would very often have to write, from the earliest invention of writing, would be personal names, which would obviously need to be entered in connection with temple receipts and ration issues. If a person delivering produce to the temple stores had a good straightforward name, which constituted a short sentence in Sumerian, there may have been no difficulty, since the elements of his name could be written with the ordinary Sumerian pictograms. Other names, however, especially if they were non-Sumerian, might well be meaningless to the scribe and so would prove impossible to write in pictograms. The only way the scribe could get round the difficulty was to divide the name up into syllables and represent each syllable by the Sumerian pictogram sounding most like that syllable. The principle was rather like taking a name such as 'Digby', which has no meaning in modern English, and representing it by pictures denoting 'dig' and 'bee'. This device was rather easier to apply widely with Sumerian than it would be with English, since most Sumerian words were of a single syllable.

A Sumerian writing sign used in this way with reference only to

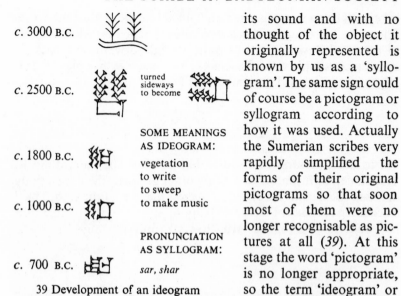

c. 3000 B.C.

c. 2500 B.C.   turned sideways to become

c. 1800 B.C.

c. 1000 B.C.

SOME MEANINGS AS IDEOGRAM:

vegetation
to write
to sweep
to make music

PRONUNCIATION AS SYLLOGRAM:

c. 700 B.C.   *sar, shar*

39 Development of an ideogram

its sound and with no thought of the object it originally represented is known by us as a 'syllogram'. The same sign could of course be a pictogram or syllogram according to how it was used. Actually the Sumerian scribes very rapidly simplified the forms of their original pictograms so that soon most of them were no longer recognisable as pictures at all (*39*). At this stage the word 'pictogram' is no longer appropriate, so the term 'ideogram' or 'logogram' is used instead. The principle remains, however, and the same sign could be an ideogram or syllogram according to how the scribe used it.

As the idea developed of using writing for more complicated matters than simple lists, the system of using syllograms was developed to give greater precision in other directions. At first, a written sentence was only a very crude approximation to the spoken sentence, since all the little elements of speech with such meanings as 'of', 'to', 'with', 'from', and so on, could not be shown. To take an example, the ideogram for 'king' was pronounced LUGALA (or possibly just LUGAL), and in actual Sumerian speech 'of the king' and 'to the king' would have been respectively LUGAL-AK and LUGALA-RA (or something very close to these forms). In the earliest writing these suffixes would have been ignored, and whether the scribe wanted to indicate 'of the king', 'to the king', or any of the other forms mentioned, he would simply have written the ideogram LUGALA and left it to the reader of the document to decide from the general situation which form was meant. (We know from our practice of omitting corresponding words in telegrams that this does not make writing unintelligible, though it certainly limits its scope.) As long as only simple things were written in Sumerian the original system caused no difficulty, but as attempts were made to write down more complicated matters, ambiguity might arise. The Sumerians, having already invented the conception of the syllogram in connection with personal names, overcame the difficulty by using the same principle. Let us suppose a Sumerian scribe wished to represent, without any possibility of ambiguity, 'to the king', LUGALA-RA. No sign yet existed for RA meaning 'to', but there was a verb RA meaning 'to hit', which had an ideogram. By using the ideogram RA 'to hit' but ignoring its original meaning and thinking only of its sound, the scribe could easily represent LUGALA-RA 'to the king'. (Once this system had become established, LUGALA-RA could not be mistaken for a sentence meaning 'the king hit', since in living Sumerian speech the latter would have several other elements, which would now have to be written out if such a sentence were intended.)

In the long run, the most important consequence of the use of syllograms was the possibility which it provided of accurately representing languages other than Sumerian. The principal language concerned here was the Semitic language which we call Akkadian. By 2500 B.C. there was a strong Semitic element in Mesopotamia, and it was a great convenience to be able to represent in writing the language of the people concerned. For simple or conventional statements, writing in ideograms would do as well for Akkadian as for Sumerian. Writing purely by ideograms could, however, become very ambiguous for more complicated statements in Akkadian, and so syllabic writing often proved essential. In consequence of the use of the syllabic principle, Akkadian was being written by 2400 B.C., and was used for quite extensive inscriptions a century later. By the Old Babylonian period (the beginning of the second millennium), Akkadian could be written in syllabic cuneiform so conveniently that we find not only· law-codes, business documents, literary works and religious compositions written in it, but also thousands of official and private letters.

Writing had begun as a means of recording economic data (receipts and issues of goods by the temple authorities) but it soon began to prove a suitable instrument for other purposes. Just as many people in our own culture collect and classify stamps or match-box labels, so also the Sumerian scribes had a passion for collecting, but what they collected and put into systematic order was data about their own civilisation, in particular their religion, their languages and their economy. Students learnt the use of cuneiform writing by copying such lists. As early as the second quarter of the third millennium the scribes were already writing catalogues of the names of gods, and of more mundane things such as animals and household objects. This process was continued and developed, ultimately giving what are in fact extensive dictionaries of Sumerian and Akkadian, which have proved of the greatest value to modern Assyriologists in increasing their understanding of those languages.

It may seem strange, but the scribes did not begin to use writing to any considerable extent for what we would call 'literature' until 1000 years after writing had first been invented. This is, however, not as odd as it at first appears. Ancient literature was something to be recited and heard, not something to be read silently. A comparison with music may make the ancient attitude clear. Music can be reduced to a score and read by anyone who has received an adequate training; but most of us would take the view that a musical composition cannot be said to have been realised unless actually played by performers. The same attitude was held by early peoples in relation to literature: it only had real existence when recited (perhaps with accompanying mime) before an audience. As long as Sumerian culture was fully living, its literature was transmitted orally from a competent reciter (perhaps employed in the Court or the temple) to his students; there was no need to write down such compositions.

Just after 2000 B.C., however, Sumerian literary compositions suddenly begin to appear in large numbers, so that about 5000 Sumerian literary tablets or fragments of tablets are now known. Our knowledge of Sumerian literature depends almost entirely on the products of this period. The reason for the changed situation is largely that the Sumerian language was rapidly becoming extinct. As a result, the literary tradition could no longer be transmitted orally as previously, and could only be reliably preserved in written form. The tendency to commit texts to writing was reinforced by the need of students to make a special study of a language which was vital to their cultural tradition, but which was no longer learnt at their mother's knee and automatically used in the business of everyday life.

For the purpose of training scribes in Sumerian there were schools. There must have been schools of some kind throughout most of the third millennium, since some of the earliest examples of writing yet found have amongst them lists of signs apparently drawn up for scribal practice. It is, however, in the first quarter of the second millennium B.C. that we have our most extensive information about scribal schools. This information comes in the form of texts written in Sumerian by people trained in those very schools, giving a detailed account of what went on in them. In the recovery and translation of these texts two modern scholars, S. N. Kramer of Philadelphia and C. J. Gadd of the British Museum and London University, stand out, and what follows is based almost entirely on their research.

It is clear in the first place that education was not in practice available to all, but was largely a privilege restricted to the children (probably only sons, though daughters were not necessarily excluded) of the wealthy and influential, who could afford to maintain their children non-productively for a long period. The examination of the parentage of several hundred scribes shows that they were all sons of such men as governors, senior civil servants, priests or scribes. An occasional poor boy or orphan might be lucky enough to be sent to school if he were adopted by a wealthy man.

It has sometimes been assumed that schools were necessarily attached to temples. This may well have been the case in some places and at some periods, but it was certainly not so for the period just after 2000 B.C. This is quite clear, because at this time such literary documents as we have all come from houses, not from temples. A number of buildings have been found which their excavators claimed, from their layout or the presence of school tablets near by, might have been school rooms. The most convincing of the buildings for which such claims have been made are two rooms, complete with benches, found at Mari (*40*).

The school was known as 'the tablet house'. We do not at present know at exactly what age formal education began. An ancient tablet refers to it as 'early youth', but except that this would probably mean at an age less than about ten, this

40 A school classroom

is not very revealing. The pupil was, at least in his early years, a day boy. He lived at home, got up at sunrise, collected his lunch from his mother, and hurried off to school. If he happened to arrive late he was duly caned, and the same fate awaited him for any misdemeanour during school hours, or for failure to perform his exercises adequately. At school education consisted of copying out texts, and probably learning them off by heart. All this appears from an actual contemporary document. The document begins with the question: 'Son of the tablet house, where did you go in your early days?' The student replies:

> I went to the tablet house; . . .
> I read out my tablet, ate my lunch,
> Prepared my (fresh) tablet, inscribed it (and) finished it . . .
> When the tablet house was dismissed, I went home.
> I entered (my) house. My father was sitting there.
> . . . I read over my tablet to him and he was pleased . . .

The Sumerian document gives some idea of the staffing of the school. At the top was the Headmaster, whose Sumerian titles meant literally 'the Expert' or 'the Father of the Tablet House'. Assisting him there was apparently a form-master, as well as specialists in particular subjects, such as Sumerian and mathematics. There seems also to have been a system of what might be called prefects or pupil-teachers, senior students called 'Big Brothers' who were responsible for knocking a certain amount of sense and Sumerian into the heads of their juniors. However, by the time the new pupil reached the middle school, and had begun to get hold of the rudiments of the scribal art, he would no longer stand in quite such awe of his 'Big Brother', and would begin to show that he had a will of his own. One of the texts amusingly shows how insubordination of this kind could cause such a disturbance that it finally called down the heavy hand of the Headmaster.

An interesting detail of school life which Professor Kramer has very recently discovered is the amount of time which the students had off each month. In a tablet from Ur a student says

> The reckoning of my monthly stay in the tablet house is (as follows):
> My days of freedom are three per month,
> Its festivals are three days per month.
> Within it, twenty-four days per month
> (Is the time of) my living in the tablet house. They are long days.

The school curriculum was long and rigorous, beginning, as we have seen, in 'early youth' (at eight or nine?) and going on to maturity. The first thing the student had to do was to become proficient in Sumerian. This involved copying out and memorising the long lists of names, technical terms, legal phrases, and so on, which had grown up in the course of the third millennium B.C. There were also texts dealing with Sumerian grammar, and others which served as dictionaries, giving Sumerian words with the Akkadian equivalents. The study of these also involved copying and memorising. Mathematics was an important part of the curriculum, for a scribe would have to know how to survey a field, or keep accounts, or calculate the number of bricks needed for a temple, or the supplies for an army.

There exists one fragment of a text which some people think is a record of a student's examination, though unfortunately its broken condition leaves the exact sense in doubt. If it is to be taken in this way, it seems that the student was first asked to write out an exercise and afterwards to inscribe his name in the special archaic script employed for inscriptions cut in stone. With this successfully achieved the student was told 'You are a scribe', and was warned against conceit. It seems likely that this particular examination was one which the student had to take before he was allowed to proceed to more advanced work. The student, having made adequate progress in the fundamentals of his craft and being now regarded as a junior scribe, could go on to study works of Sumerian literature, and might possibly even attempt to produce original compositions.

Not all scribes, of course, acquired the same degree of competence. Some might be able to do no more than write out contracts or letters, which normally employed largely syllabic writings and would be relatively easy for a Babylonian or Assyrian trained to write in cuneiform. At the other end of the scribal scale would be the men able to deal with difficult religious texts, some of whom produced texts which, either from the extensive use of rare ideograms, or the employment of a difficult style or rare words, have not yet been fully elucidated by modern experts.

Once qualified, scribes (as a class) had a wide range of possible professions awaiting them, though the actual choice open to any particular scribe was very much limited, and would probably be largely settled by his family connections. Indeed, it was regarded as decreed by the god Enlil that a man should follow his father's profession. Probably all classes of priests received an initial training as scribes, though as the qualifications for the priesthood were more rigorous than those for scribal training, not every category of priesthood was open to every scribe. Diviners, for example, had to be of good birth and good physique, as indeed did anyone with any office in the temple, even in the first millennium B.C. Broken teeth, a squint or a limp or any such disability would disqualify a man for such offices.

Amongst the men at the top of the scribal profession were the high-ranking priests who presided at the great temple festivals: there are known a number of the rituals which they made use of in the course of their duties, and these texts, largely written in ideograms which served to make the understanding of them more difficult to anyone who had not been trained in this type of text generally contain a final note to the effect that only the initiated shall be allowed to see it.

Since so many commercial transactions required an accompanying written document, most scribes must have been concerned mainly with activities of this kind. One may probably think of some of them as sitting in the market-place ready to assist in any business transactions taking place. Others were in government or temple service. Any official of importance, whether serving the temples or the King, would have one or more scribes on his staff, accompanying him and ready to take down memoranda, or to do the necessary

calculations in connection with assessments of taxes, ration issues and so on. A Babylonian official without a scribe was as handicapped as a modern business executive when his private secretary goes sick. In a letter of the sixth century we find a temple official, writing from some outlying part of the temple estates to the central administration, saying, 'As to the 200 hired men for whom I am responsible, though I brought the silver and wool (for their wages), I could not

41 Assyrian writing boards

issue it to them without a scribe. The scribe and the (account) list are there with you.' Since this official had managed to have the letter written from which we have quoted, we have to conclude either that officials sometimes wrote their own letters, or that there was a strict division of function between different classes of scribes, so that one available for correspondence could not be expected to work out calculations of ration issues for which another man was responsible.

42 Scribes

Scribes also accompanied military expeditions. Commanders would need scribes to write dispatches home, and we have in fact many letters actually written from a battlefield, including one which is specifically said to have been written during the very engagement when the great gate of Babylon was being forced, during the reign of Tiglath-Pileser III. Scribes were also needed by the army both as quartermasters for the issue of rations and equipment and as accountants for the listing of booty. Several bas-reliefs show scribes noting down the claims of Assyrian warriors as to their prowess in battle and the number of their victims (42); some of these bas-reliefs make it appear that one of the scribes is writing on a clay tablet, whilst another is using some material, either parchment or papyrus, in scroll form. Another writing medium sometimes used for cuneiform script consisted of ivory boards with a coating of wax soft enough to take the impression of a stylus; a series of such boards might be hinged together (41).

Another profession which required some scribal training was that of medicine. Doctors had to be literate, as there were collections of medical documents on clay tablets which were obviously their textbooks. The copies known to us mostly date from after 1000 B.C. but they can be shown to go back to originals from the Old Babylonian period (early second millennium). These medical documents were made up mainly of lists of symptoms and prescriptions. The symptoms are listed in the form 'If a man has a pain in his belly' (or some other part of his body), and the text then goes into details of the patient's trouble. The kind of things that might be mentioned were whether the man's skin felt hot or cold, whether his pulse was rapid or his veins swollen, whether there was any inflammation or redness or whether the patient had a cough or a headache or felt dizzy. There then followed a note on the appropriate treatment. Various herbs or minerals might be used, and could be administered in various ways. They might be mixed with something such as beer and then swallowed, or applied in the form of a lotion or an ointment or even as an enema.

Details of such surgery as the Babylonian and Assyrian doctors were capable of performing seem never to have been committed to writing by the scribes, and we know very little about this.

An important part of the curriculum in the scribal schools was mathematics, and it was in the Old Babylonian period, the period at which we are best acquainted with the scribal schools, that Babylonian mathematics reached a pinnacle of achievement which was not to be attained again until another millennium and a half had passed.

The Sumerians had, at the very beginning of writing, already devised symbols for numerals and two systems of counting, one (the decimal) based on ten as the unit, and the other (the sexagesimal) based on sixty. The two systems were not mutually exclusive, and in ordinary use both were employed together without causing any confusion, just as alongside the decimal system we use (for money and linear measurement) a system based on twelve.

By the Old Babylonian period the forms of the symbols used for numbers were as follows

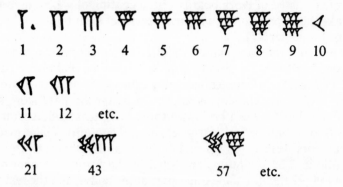

At some periods and in some types of text 60 was denoted by the sign ⌶ . This is, of course, the same sign as that for 1, and it might be thought that this would have led to endless confusion. A

comparison with our own system of numerals will show that this was not necessarily so. Our symbol for 'ten' is precisely the same as our symbol for 'one', namely '1'. It is true that if we want to indicate exactly ten we put a nought after it, but the nought symbol does not occur in any other number in the 'ten' series. It is the '1' (placed in a special position) which is the vital part of the symbol for 'ten', not the whole group '10'; if the '0' were an essential part of the 'ten' symbol we should for 'fifteen' have to write 105 (which is exactly what small children do before they understand our numeral system). 'Fifteen' and 'fifty-one' in our system use exactly the same symbols, but in a different order. It was the use of a corresponding system (the ancestor of our own, in fact) which saved the Babylonians from being confused by ϒ to denote either 'one' or 'sixty'. The convention was that ϡ denoted 'sixty plus ten' (*i.e.* seventy), whereas ⟨ϒ meant 'ten plus one' (*i.e.* eleven).

'One hundred' could be represented as 'sixty plus forty', according to the system above, or written with the sign ϯ, pronounced *me*, which is simply a form of the Semitic word for 'hundred'. There was a special sign for '1000', and another for 3600, which is 60 × 60 and so the highest term in the sexagesimal system.

Babylonian mathematical methods were basically algebraic, and the Babylonian mathematicians of the Old Babylonian period were able to calculate such values of numbers as square roots and cube roots, of which tables have been found, and to solve quadratic equations.

There follows an example of an actual problem on an Old Babylonian clay tablet, with its solution. The text reads:

I have added the surface of my two squares: 28;20.
(The side of) one square is a quarter (the side of) the (other) square.
You put down 4 and 1.
You multiply 4 by 4: 16.
You multiply 1 by 1: 1.
You add 1 and 16:   17.
The reciprocal of 17 cannot be solved.
What must I put to 17 [*i.e.* What must I multiply 17 by] which will give me 28;20? 1;40.
This is the square of 10.
You raise 10 by 4 and 40 is (the side of) one square.
You raise 10 by 1 and 10 is (the side of) the second square.

The Babylonian solution of this problem is much simpler than the literal translation at first suggests. It can be explained by using modern algebraic symbols, though it must be emphasised that though this follows the way in which the Babylonian probably thought, it does not follow the way in which he wrote it down.

The number 28;20 is written in the sexagesimal system, that is, the '20' represents twenty times one, and the '28' represents twenty-eight times sixty. The 'surface' of the squares means their area.

Let us call the length of the side of the larger square x, and of the smaller square y. The data therefore gives us the equations:

$$x^2 + y^2 = 28;20$$
$$x = 4y$$

Take y as $1n$

$$\text{Then } x = 4n$$
$$x^2 = 16n^2$$
$$y^2 = 1n^2$$
$$\therefore \quad x^2 + y^2 = 17n^2 = 28;20$$
$$\therefore \quad n^2 = \frac{28;20}{17} = 1;40$$
$$n = 10$$
$$\therefore \quad x = 10 \times 4 = 40$$
$$y = 10 \times 1 = 10$$

As to their geometrical knowledge, it may be mentioned that the Babylonian mathematicians knew the value of π very accurately, taking it as $3\frac{1}{8}$. Some cuneiform tablets are known which deal with the areas of geometrical figures (45).

Another of the Babylonian scribal activities, related to mathematics, was astronomy. The Babylonians had two reasons for paying particular attention to the movements of the heavenly bodies. One was the need to regulate the calendar so that agricultural operations could be efficiently planned, and the other was the theory that events upon earth were either a reflection of, or at least directly related to, events in the sky. In the sky, in fact, the Babylonians thought they could actually see what the gods were doing. As early as the Old Babylonian period we have lists of observations of Venus covering several years. Eclipses of sun and moon could not fail to be noticed, and were recorded, at least spasmodically, from an early date. From the middle of the eighth century B.C. (precisely 747 B.C. according to a Greek astronomer

43 Archaic clay tablet
From Erech, c. *3000* B.C.

44 Cuneiform tablet
From El Amarna, c. *1400* B.C.

45 Geometrical tablet
From Babylonia, c. *1700* B.C.

46 Babylonian cylinder-seal impression
Agade Dynasty, c. *2350* B.C.

47 Assyrian cylinder-seal impression, *c.* 700 B.C.

of nine centuries later) systematic records of eclipses were kept, and these records, extending over centuries, eventually made it possible to calculate the movements (or apparent movements) of the sun, moon and planets relative to each other and across the sky. The details of this are, however, too complex and difficult to discuss here.

The scribal activity most likely to find an echo in modern man is ancient Mesopotamian literature (the word being used here in its narrow sense of something worth reading, not something which happened to be written). Much of this has been preserved for us in the great library collected at Nineveh by Ashurbanipal and his predecessors, but other important works, both in Sumerian and Akkadian, have been found at a number of other sites, some of them far outside the boundaries of ancient Babylonia or Assyria.

The best known of these ancient literary works is the *Epic of Gilgamesh*, available in several translations in English, some good, others less than good. We do not know who composed this any more than (with one possible exception) we know who composed any other piece of ancient Mesopotamian literature. There were, indeed, at least four or five older Sumerian stories about Gilgamesh in circulation. The underlying Sumerian stories are separate tales dealing with different aspects of the traditions of Gilgamesh. The Babylonian poet has integrated these Sumerian compositions and created a tragedy, a single story which moves relentlessly forward to its final conclusion, that man's lot has been decreed by the gods, and that man is powerless to resist the working of the divinely ordained order.

Gilgamesh was a priest-king of the city of Uruk (Biblical Erech) in the Early Dynastic period (about 2600 B.C.). This period was in the very shadow-land of tradition, and beyond it lay the period of the gods, so that Gilgamesh himself was said to be two-thirds divine.

According to a fragment of the epic in Hittite, Gilgamesh was of gigantic proportions; his height was about sixteen feet and his chest measurement in proportion (*49*). As the story begins Gilgamesh, likened to a wild bull, and described as the shepherd of Uruk, is acting oppressively towards his fellow-citizens.

The gods considered the matter, and ordered the goddess Aruru to make a rival to him. This she did, in the form of a wild man Enkidu, whom she placed in the steppe-land, where he lived with the beasts of the field. There a hunter saw him, and reported to his

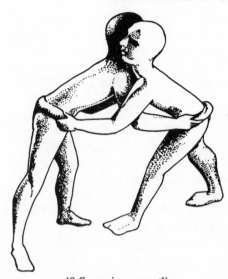

48 Sumerians wrestling

father that this formidable creature was making it impossible for him to catch the game. The matter finally came to Gilgamesh, who decided to send a prostitute to ensnare Enkidu. The hunter took the lady to the watering-place in the steppe-land, where she awaited the coming of Enkidu with the animals. As soon as the wild man arrived, the prostitute exposed herself to him; Enkidu fell in love with her, and they made love together for six days and seven nights.

But when Enkidu, his desire at last satiated, sought to join the wild beasts again, they fled from him. Perforce Enkidu had to go back to the woman, who persuaded him to return with her to Uruk. She described the splendour of city life, and inspired in him a desire to meet Gilgamesh. Meanwhile in Uruk the Sun-god had sent to Gilgamesh a dream, foretelling the coming from the steppe-land of one like himself, who should become his comrade. Enkidu entered the city, challenged Gilgamesh, and wrestled with him:

> They met in the market-place of the land.
> Enkidu barred the gate with his foot,
> And would not allow Gilgamesh to enter.
> They grappled with each other, butting like bulls.
> They shattered the doorpost, so that the wall trembled.
> . . . .
> As Gilgamesh bent his knee, with his foot still on the ground,
> His rage left him, and he turned away.
> When he had turned away, Enkidu said to him, to Gilgamesh,
> '. . . . .
> Your head is raised above (all other) men;
> Enlil has granted you the kingship over the people.'

The two became fast friends.

The idea now came to Gilgamesh of going to the cedar forest to destroy the monster Huwawa (or Humbaba), whom the god Enlil had appointed to protect the forest against mankind. (In economic terms one may perhaps interpret this as the beginning of the large-scale exploitation of the forests of the Zagros.) Enkidu attempted to dissuade his friend, though without success, and the two, armed with great axes and swords which no ordinary man could even lift, set off, after duly consulting the omens.

At last the heroes reached the forest, which struck them with awe:

> They stood, and they gazed at the forest;
> They kept looking at the height of the cedars,
> They kept looking at the entrance to the forest.
> Where Humbaba used to walk there was a path made;
> The tracks ran straight; the way was well looked after.
> They saw the cedar mountain, the dwelling place of the gods, the throne of the goddess Irnini.

The heroes rested for the night, and in the morning they entered the forest and began to fell the cedars. This aroused and enraged the guardian Humbaba, but with the aid of his patron the Sun-god, Gilgamesh was able to overcome him.

The text is broken at this point. Where it resumes, the scene has shifted back to Uruk, where Gilgamesh, cleansed from his journey, has put on his most splendid raiment. Ishtar, the goddess of love(*50*), was overcome by the sight of his virile beauty, and offered herself to him, with the promise of luxury, wealth, and pre-eminence amongst rulers. Gilgamesh

49 Gilgamesh (?) subduing a lion

89

50 Ishtar, goddess of Love

rejected the offer, narrating somewhat caddishly the fate of previous lovers of Ishtar. The rejected goddess went off in a rage to her father Anu, the supreme god, and complained to him

My father, Gilgamesh keeps pouring insults upon me,

and by means of threats induced her father to create the Bull of Heaven to destroy Gilgamesh. But terrible as the bull was to ordinary men, Enkidu seems to have vaulted over the bull's horns (in a manner often depicted in Minoan art, 85) and grasped it by the thick of the tail. The point of this was presumably to steer the brute into a position where Gilgamesh could finish it off. Gilgamesh managed to drive his dagger into the upper part of the monster's neck, and so killed it. Ishtar, watching from the walls of the city, shrieked out a curse and assembled all the temple-women in lamentation. For Gilgamesh and Enkidu, however, this was a time of triumph, and they rode (presumably on donkeys, since horses were not yet known in Mesopotamia) through ranks of admiring citizens lining the streets of Uruk. A great celebration followed. But in the night Enkidu had a dream, in which he saw the gods in council. The supreme three, Anu, Enlil and Ea, together with the Sun-god Shamash, the patron of Gilgamesh, discussed the matter, and despite the opposition of Shamash decreed that, because of the killing of Humbaba and the Heavenly Bull, Enkidu must die. Enkidu fell ill, and as the end approached he regretted the events which had taken him from the steppe-land, and called down curses on the hunter and the prostitute. But the Sun-god pointed out the blessings of civilisation to which the prostitute had brought him, and Enkidu became calm, and turned his curse to a blessing. Before he died Enkidu had another dream, in which there was revealed to him the nature of the Underworld, the place of the Afterlife. In the dream, said Enkidu, he was met by a being who changed him so that his arms were covered with feathers like those

90

of a bird. His guide took him down to a house of gloom, a house from which the person who enters never comes forth, from which there is no road back. Here the people were all like birds, and lived in gloom, with dust and clay as their food.

Finally Enkidu died. Gilgamesh lamented bitterly over his friend, and performed for him the appropriate last rites. Then there came upon Gilgamesh the realisation that he too must in the end die like Enkidu. Like every man, when this truth first came to him he could not accept it, and sought a means by which to avoid the human lot. There was a primeval ancestor, Uta-napishtim, who had escaped mortality, and to him Gilgamesh would go, to learn his secret.

Gilgamesh walked to the mountains of Mashu, which the Sumerians thought of as forming a ring round the earth, and reached one of the gates at the edge of the world provided for the rising and setting of the sun. The scorpion-people (*51*), appointed as guards, recognised him as part divine, and allowed Gilgamesh to pass. He travelled on through thick darkness for eleven hours, and then at last the dawn broke. In another two hours he came into the full light of day, and found himself in a garden with trees bearing precious stones. Here he met the friendly Sun-god, who warned him that his quest would be without avail. But Gilgamesh went on, and presently came to the lady Siduri, who kept the inn at the edge of the Abyss. She received him kindly, but warned him that no one but the Sun-god could ever cross that sea. Nevertheless Uta-napishtim had a ferryman, Urshanabi, at present in the woods near by, and by his help Gilgamesh might cross. Gilgamesh met Urshanabi, who instructed Gilgamesh what to do. It was necessary to punt across the centre of the Abyss, but the waters there were waters of death, and no drop must touch Gilgamesh. Therefore Gilgamesh was

51 A scorpion-man

91

instructed to cut down 120 trees and prepare them as punting poles. The two embarked, and when they reached the danger area Urshanabi ordered Gilgamesh to punt, using each pole once only to avoid contact with the waters of death. When the last pole had been used the boat reached safe waters, within sight of Uta-napishtim, who looked in amazement at the unexpected stranger. Upon arrival Gilgamesh gave an account of himself and his desire to avoid death. Uta-napishtim in reply pointed out the impermanence of all human life and institutions, but Gilgamesh pointed out:

> I keep looking at you, Uta-napishtim,
> Your appearance is no different, you are like me;
> And you yourself are not different, you are like me;
> . . . .
> Tell me how it is that you stand in the assembly of the gods, (and) have life.

Uta-napishtim thereupon gave Gilgamesh the story of the Deluge, which had resulted in his being granted eternal life. He had lived in the city of Shurippak on the Euphrates. The gods decided to permit Enlil to destroy mankind by a great flood, but the god Ea, however, revealed the secret to Uta-napishtim by whispering to the reed-hut in which the hero slept, and gave instructions for the making of a ship. Uta-napishtim had the ship built and provisioned, and filled it not only with specimens of all living creatures, as in the Biblical story of Noah, but also with craftsmen: the Sumerians realised that without craftsmen civilisation as they knew it would be impossible. At last the heavens and the subterranean water channels were opened, there was a great tempest, and the whole earth and everything on it was submerged and drowned. Even the gods were terrified and fled to the highest heaven. When the destruction was complete, the storm abated, and the ship grounded on a mountain. Uta-napishtim, like Noah, sent out birds to seek for dry land, and at last he knew that the waters had subsided sufficiently for him to release his cargo of animals and to leave the ship. He himself offered a sacrifice upon the mountain, and the hungry gods, who had received no smoke offering since the flood began, came clustering round. But Enlil was furious that his plan for the total destruction of mankind had not been carried through. Ea, however, succeeded in calming the angry god by pointing out that there were other means of controlling mankind than total destruction; were there not wild beasts, famine and disease to control the population? The divine wrath should not be indiscriminate but should have a moral basis:

> On the sinner impose his sin; on the transgressor impose his transgression.

Enlil saw the reasonableness of this, went into the ship and called Uta-napishtim and his wife to him. Then, as Uta-napishtim described it,

> He touched our foreheads and stood between us (and) blessed us,
> (Saying) 'Formerly Uta-napishtim was human.
> Now Uta-napishtim and his wife shall become gods, like us.
> Uta-napishtim shall dwell far away, at the mouth of the rivers.'
> They took me and let me dwell far away, at the mouth of the rivers.

Uta-napishtim went on to point out that there was no one to do this for Gilgamesh, and challenged him to show himself able to conquer his human frailty in even such a small matter as being able to resist sleep for six days and seven nights. But even as he sat there, Gilgamesh, exhausted from his wandering, succumbed to a heavy sleep. Uta-napishtim realised that Gilgamesh would claim only to have fallen into a brief doze, and so set his wife to bake bread each day and set it beside the sleeping hero. This she did, and when Gilgamesh awoke and began to excuse himself for what he thought had been a short nap, Uta-napishtim pointed out the heaps of bread to him. There it was, in all stages from bread still cooking on the coals, through bread that was beginning to go mouldy, to dried-up crusts of a week ago. Gilgamesh was compelled to acknowledge his failure, and to accept his human lot. Uta-napishtim told the ferryman Urshanabi to wash Gilgamesh and give him new clothing, and then take him back to Uruk. But just as the wanderer was leaving, the wife of Uta-napishtim persuaded her husband not to let him go back empty-handed, whereupon Uta-napishtim gave him the secret of a magic plant with thorns, called 'Old-man-becomes-young', growing at the bottom of the sea. This plant would give Gilgamesh eternal youth. In the manner of a pearl-diver Gilgamesh fixed heavy stones to himself, which dragged him down to the bottom of the water. There he found the plant, and, cutting off the stones which held him down, was thrown up on to the shore, where he continued his journey, by land, still accompanied by Urshanabi. But even after obtaining the magic plant

Gilgamesh was to be frustrated. On the way home the hero stopped to bathe in a pool of cold water, and in his absence a snake came and stole the plant. Gilgamesh bitterly lamented his total failure to alter his human lot of old age and death, and returned with Urshanabi empty-handed to Uruk. But if he had lost the possibility of escape from the human lot, Gilgamesh could still rejoice in the sight of human achievements, and we finally see him pointing out to Urshanabi the splendours of Uruk, the great centre of early Sumerian civilisation.

Amongst the other better preserved epics extant in Akkadian are the *Epic of Adapa* and the *Epic of Etana*. Adapa was a fisherman in the service of Ea, the Water-god who was also god of Wisdom and patron of the city of Eridu. Some scholars have tried, not very convincingly, to relate the name 'Adapa' to the Biblical name 'Adam'. One day Adapa was out in his boat fishing, when the south wind gave him a ducking. In revenge, Adapa, by a magical spell which he had no doubt learnt in the service of Ea, broke the wing of the south wind, which could then no longer blow. After a week the supreme god Anu noticed the absence of the south wind and made enquiries. Upon learning the facts, he gave orders for Adapa to appear before him in heaven. Ea took care, however, that Adapa did not go without the benefit of his advice and inside knowledge. Adapa was to put on mourning, and when questioned on this by the two door-keepers of heaven he was to reply that he was in mourning for two gods who had disappeared from the earth. Since the two door-keepers were the gods in question this would at once gain Adapa their good word. Moreover, Anu would offer Adapa bread and water which were the bread and water of death; these he must on no account eat or drink.

The first part of Ea's plan was successful. Adapa explained that since the south wind had capsized him without warning he had had a severe provocation. The two divine door-keepers, duly flattered at Adapa's respect for their memory, also put in a good word for Adapa, and Anu was won over. Deciding to grant Adapa immortality, he offered him not, as Ea had anticipated, the bread and water of death but the bread and water of life. Unaware of the true nature of the food Anu was offering, and remembering Ea's advice, Adapa refused to eat or drink. Anu, recognising what was in Adapa's mind, laughed at him, and telling him that by his refusal he had thrown away the chance of immortality, sent him back to earth.

The other epic mentioned, the *Epic of Etana*, is related to acceptance in early Sumerian thought of hereditary kingship as one of the values of civilisation. To give mankind security, the gods had sent kingship down from heaven, and settled it upon the pious Etana. But Etana had no heir, even though he sacrificed daily to the Sun-god Shamash. Shamash arranged for Etana to befriend an eagle who had fallen foul of a serpent, and the grateful eagle carried Etana up to heaven in quest of the plant of birth. At present we do not know how the epic ended, but a new edition of the text is in preparation by J. V. Kinnier Wilson of Cambridge University, who has found some important new sections.

52 Etana riding on an eagle

There is space only for a passing reference to other epics and myths known, more or less completely, in Akkadian or Sumerian versions. There are, for example, quite a number of fragments of myths of creation. Another quaint little myth explains the origin of toothache: it was due to a worm which at the Creation objected to having fruit as its food and asked the gods to allow it to suck the gums at the roots of the teeth. Another myth, known after its hero as *Atrakhasis*, is in part parallel to the Deluge story. The *Myth of Zu* concerns the attempt of a minor Bird-god called Zu (or possibly Anzu) to gain supremacy in the pantheon by stealing an insignia called the Tablets of Destiny: after initial success Zu (or Anzu) was pursued and defeated by another god. A myth known as the *Myth of Erra* was specially related to the city of Babylon and the recital of this myth served, it was believed, to ward off epidemics. There are also important epics containing traditions of the dynasty of Agade, including one dealing with the birth and upbringing of Sargon of Agade himself.

Purely Sumerian myths, though of great interest in themselves, lie outside the scope of the present book. The reader who is interested in these will find a most readable and authoritative account of them in S. N. Kramer's *Sumerian Mythology* (Harper Torchbooks, 1961).

A class of literature quite different from what we have been discussing is that which we know as Wisdom Literature. This category will be familiar to most readers, since there are examples of it in the Bible, in the books of *Proverbs*, *Job* and *Ecclesiastes*. Wisdom Literature ranged from earthy proverbial sayings bandied about amongst peasants to highly sophisticated discussions of what we should call philosophical or theological problems. The kind of problems discussed were aspects of the questions, what is the purpose of life and why does seemingly unmerited suffering occur? There were three major works on these themes in Akkadian, though scarcely any traces in Sumerian. The most striking of the compositions of this kind was the poem called in Akkadian *Ludlul bel nemeqi* ('I will praise the Lord of Wisdom'), often referred to as 'The Poem of the Righteous Sufferer'. This had the same basic theme as the *Book of Job*, that is, it concerned a man who, for no fault of his own, was apparently deserted by the divine powers and handed over to the powers of evil.

The proverbs mentioned are sometimes very obscure and (like our own) often difficult to understand if their application is not known. None the less there are quite a few which are self-explanatory, the following among them:

Eat no fat, and you won't excrete blood.

A scorpion stung a man. What did he receive (for it)?
An informer caused a man's death. (By) what did he benefit?

She's pregnant without intercourse, 'tis said;
It's by not eating she has put on weight!

If I am to die, let me eat (my savings);
If I am to live, let me put (money) by.

One of the most interesting pieces of Akkadian literature is of quite a different kind from any yet mentioned. It is in fact a humorous composition. This has only been excavated in the last few years, and so far is unique of its kind in literature written in cuneiform.

The story concerned a man named Gimil-Ninurta, 'poor and lowly', living in the city of Nippur. He had no silver or gold, and his face was pinched for want of food and drink. Finally he decided to sell his clothes and buy a goat. He could have eaten the goat himself, but to feast alone was a grave social offence, and he still lacked the beer which guests would expect. Thinking the matter over, he concluded that the best plan would be to present the goat to the Mayor, on the principle, no doubt, that once he had gained the Mayor's goodwill he would profit by his gift many times over. But things did not work out in that way. The Mayor kept the goat, but then flew into a rage, accusing Gimil-Ninurta of attempted bribery, and had him shown to the door. Gimil-Ninurta was understandably annoyed and, through the gate-keeper, promised the Mayor to pay him for the insult three times over. But this seemed an empty threat and, as the text says, 'When the Mayor heard (this) he laughed all day.'

Gimil-Ninurta went straight off to the King, kissed the ground before him, and made his request. He asked that the King should lend him a chariot for a single day, in return for which he would give a mina of gold. The King agreed, and Gimil-Ninurta was provided with a chariot and a robe as though he had been a noble-man. Gimil-Ninurta then made his way back to the residence of the Mayor of Nippur, taking with him an empty treasure-chest. The Mayor came out to welcome the supposed royal messenger, who claimed to be taking gold to the temple for the King. In the middle of the night Gimil-Ninurta got up, opened his treasure-chest, and set up an outcry that he had been robbed. He set upon the Mayor so violently that the latter finally gave him two minas of gold in settlement for that which had supposedly been stolen within his house. As Gimil-Ninurta moved off in his chariot he told the gate-keeper: 'Tell your master, "I have settled one score with you." '

Gimil-Ninurta now took himself to have his head shaved and, thus disguised, returned to the Mayor's residence and made him-self out to be a doctor from the city of Isin. He was admitted, and the Mayor showed him the bruises he had received from the supposed royal messenger. The bedside manner of the bogus doctor apparently inspired confidence, and when he told the Mayor that his cures worked best in darkness the Mayor took him into a private room. Gimil-Ninurta, who had brought with him, as part of his supposed medical equipment, a vessel of water and fire in some form, poured the water over the fire and in the resulting darkness trussed up the Mayor and beat him up. He then left, remarking to the gate-keeper as he went that he had settled the second score.

By now, however, the Mayor had put two and two together and realised that the man who had given him the goat was behind his recent troubles, and gave orders to all his staff to keep a special watch for the fellow. Knowing this, Gimil-Ninurta hid himself under a bridge near the Mayor's residence, and arranged for a man to shout 'Here is the man with the goat.' The whole of the Mayor's staff went rushing off to catch 'the man with the goat', leaving the Mayor alone. Gimil-Ninurta jumped out from his hiding-place, grabbed the Mayor, and gave him his third beating up. Satisfied that justice had now been done, Gimil-Ninurta went off to the country, leaving the unfortunate Mayor more dead than alive.

Chapter V

RUNNING AN EMPIRE

AMONGST all the aspects of ancient Mesopotamian life, there are few which have been more widely misunderstood and misrepresented than the nature of Assyrian imperialism. Few historians or other writers who touch upon Assyria in the period between 900 B.C. and its final fall just before 600 B.C. can resist the temptation to gather up their skirts and add yet another shocked comment upon the barbarism, brutality and unmatched ruthlessness of the Assyrians. It is rare to find any attempt to look at Assyrian warfare and imperialism as a whole in its perspective. Yet, as it is hoped to show below, when one considers the whole functioning of the Assyrian Empire, and particularly when one passes judgement in accordance with the standards, not of our own times but of the other peoples of the ancient world, a very different picture emerges. The Assyrian Empire was efficient and would not gladly bear with those who wished to upset the civilised order, but it was not exceptionally bloody or barbaric. The number of people killed or mutilated in an average Assyrian campaign in the interest of efficient administration was, even in proportion to the population, probably no more than the number of dead and mangled humans that most Western countries offer annually as a sacrifice to the motor-car, in the supposed interest of efficient transport.

An account of the general framework of history in which the Assyrian Empire grew, flourished, and finally collapsed will be found above (pp. 41–52). This framework can be filled out considerably with details of the day-to-day activities of the various officials of the Empire. At most periods there was a very tight control of affairs by the central government at the capital, so that the King (or his ministers) required frequent and detailed reports from provincial officials on all aspects of administration. Nearly 2000 of the letters which passed between provincial officials and the authorities at the capital have now been found, and letters such as these often enable us to fill out the bare outline of events which the royal annals and similar documents give us.

In trying to obtain a glimpse of the Empire in action, it would be instructive if we were able to follow up the career of a single typical official. Unfortunately, there is no single official of whom we have sufficient details to give us a complete picture of an administrator's life. On the other hand, there are many officials of whom we know one or two isolated incidents, and taken together these isolated incidents make it possible to build up a fairly complete composite picture. Such a composite picture is attempted below: it must be stressed that what follows is not offered as the biography of any individual actually known to us, and to that extent it may be considered imaginary. But though imaginary, it need not be considered fictitious, since every significant event mentioned below is actually known to have happened to some administrator or other.

Our typical official, whom we shall call Qurdi-Ashur-lamur, was born of an Assyrian father who held land from the King in the district around the ancient city of Ashur, in former times the capital. The family had lived there for generations, and each new heir had the estates granted to him afresh (upon payment of substantial presents) by the reigning monarch. The members of the family had loyally performed their part in the royal service, and in

53 Men carrying hares, locusts and fruit

the family burial ground there were regular offerings of food and beer at the tombs of ancestors who had died fighting for the King.

Qurdi-Ashur-lamur's mother had been the only wife of his father, monogamy being the normal form of marriage in Assyria at this time. She was assisted at Qurdi-Ashur-lamur's birth by a midwife, who sought to ease the pains of the mother's labour by practical measures

54 Assyrian boy shooting at a target

and magical rituals, such as one which told of two good spirits descending from heaven with holy water and oil. In the rituals the midwife may have been assisted by a priest. After the necessary practical steps and magical hocus-pocus had been completed, the father was admitted to the bedroom, where he held his son, thereby accepting his legitimacy. The mother suckled her son for the best part of two years; perhaps this was the reason that during that time she had no further children.

As soon as Qurdi-Ashur-lamur was old enough to toddle about behind his father he was taught to sit a horse. A little later he was introduced to the use of the bow, and thereafter spent much of his childhood shooting at targets in competition with his friends or amusing himself in the pursuit of small game (54). At some time before the age of ten he found this freedom disagreeably checked, when he was put into the charge of a prosy old priest or local scribe to learn the rudiments of the cuneiform script. No one expected him to master the higher flights of the scribal art, but it was essential for his future career that he should at least be able to write letters and deal with accounts. But formal education alone was by no means the decisive factor in ensuring a successful career, and Qurdi-Ashur-lamur's father, himself with an honourable record of service to the royal family, was careful to keep up his contacts at Court. At a favourable opportunity the father sent off a worthy

55 A foreigner bringing tribute to Assyria

present and asked for a word to be dropped in the right quarter: 'gifts of money made their way to the right officials, and finally Qurdi-Ashur-lamur received an appointment as a page at the royal Court.

If Qurdi-Ashur-lamur did not find plenty to interest him at Court, he must have been either a very dull or a very disagreeable young man. Though his duties all centred around the King, there was a good deal of variety in the things he and the other young men like him actually did. Periodically vassal rulers and their representatives made visits to the Assyrian King, and on these occasions Qurdi-Ashur-lamur, with some of the other young men, might be in attendance. Often these were routine occasions, but sometimes there were excitements, as when a ruler from a distant land sent presents of unusual creatures, such as an elephant, a crocodile, or two-humped camels.

Another excitement would be when the victorious Assyrian army returned from campaign laden with booty. There would be a procession through the capital to the chief temple, and after the King had presented his report to the god and made dedications, some of the booty would be installed within the palace, perhaps fine gold or bronze vessels from Urartu (Armenia) or carved ivory furniture from Syria. In the time of Ashurbanipal two obelisks were once brought back from Egypt to be displayed in the capital.

Inside the palace, it is likely that amongst their other duties the pages served the King at meals, but their really important task was to act, as one King put it, as the 'brighteners of the royal mind'. Exactly how they set about brightening the royal mind we do not know, but presumably their presence and liveliness served to counteract the possibly depressing effect of the ponderous Court ritual and the gravity of the leading religious functionaries and ministers. Certainly the King must often have needed cheering up, for, to say nothing of the prosiness which must have been a characteristic of men who had gone through the full course of the scribal

curriculum, the King was often put to great personal inconvenience. There were occasions when the priests claimed to have seen
menacing omens, and the King might then be made to fast for
several days, or be obliged to keep away from his womenfolk, or
even have to be shaved all over.

One of the royal religious duties which, whatever the King may
have thought of it privately, certainly did not cause him tedium,
was the royal lion hunt. At this event, lions were released from
cages in an enclosed park to be ritually shot down by the King or
even killed by his dagger (56). Needless to say, there were seasoned
bowmen near at hand to prevent any serious mishap to the King,
but this responsibility is not likely to have fallen to green young
men like Qurdi-Ashur-lamur and his companions. They may well
have been among the beaters, or even in a place of safety among
the spectators behind a line of spearsmen. Some of the lions were
wild ones straight from the mountains, whilst others were actually
bred from cubs which had been caught and sent to the capital
specially for this purpose. Lions were not the only animals kept

56 Ashurbanipal killing a lion

in captivity at the Assyrian capital: some of the kings had quite a zoo, with such animals as gazelles, deer, wild asses, leopards, bears, wild oxen, and elephants, which the people were allowed to see. It is likely, though not certain, that some of these animals were also released in a park to be shot down, like the lions.

Alongside such diversions Qurdi-Ashur-lamur's education continued, though by informal rather than formal means. He might be present to hear the debates of the King's ministers and the advice given by the royal astrologers after consulting the omens, and dull and pompous though such things might appear at the time, they would do much to open the young man's mind to the wider aspects of both imperial and religious affairs. Probably it was not consciously recognised, even by those directly concerned, but the King was governed by the omens, and the omens were governed by the priests; so that in effect a committee of the most intelligent, learned, and level-headed men in the kingdom had the power of veto over any ill-considered plan put forward by the King.

Further broadening of Qurdi-Ashur-lamur's mind would come from his day-to-day mixing with the other boys at Court. Of these, some would be Assyrian like himself, others the sons of foreign vassals who had been sent to Court as hostages. From the latter a young Assyrian might acquire a smattering of some of the foreign languages of the Empire, and afterwards, if he found himself interested enough to wish to go further, he could receive more formal instruction by making friends with one of the interpreters at Court.

By the time Qurdi-Ashur-lamur was in his late teens, he might be permitted to accompany the King as he went on campaign, either running by his chariot together with other young men of the same status, or perhaps serving as a cavalryman. He would now have his first sight of warfare. The army would make its advance, as described later in this chapter, into territory unfamiliar to Qurdi-Ashur-lamur, until it reached a valley from which, perhaps, there had come reports that all was not well. In the valley the local ruler would come hurrying with his courtiers and sons to bow low before the King, offering gifts as a token of loyalty. The ruler would be given a feast and confirmed in his little princedom by his Assyrian overlord, and his ministers would tell the Assyrian King what they knew of developments among their neighbours. They might mention particularly a series of troublesome raids from the mountain folk, who had recently been receiving with considerable enthusiasm a mission from Urartu, the powerful kingdom in Armenia. At the same time the vassal prince would perhaps also introduce his heir, in the hope of receiving the promise of the Assyrian King to support him as the lawful successor if treason or external attack brought about the death of the vassal prince himself.

It would be usual in the circumstances imagined for a contingent of the army to be sent to the mountains to investigate the complaint of anti-Assyrian activity, and Qurdi-Ashur-lamur might accompany the soldiers. As the troops reached the first of the mountain villages they would be likely to find it deserted except for a few old men and women incapable of leaving, a clear indication that there was some justification for the charges against the hillsmen. High above them, the Assyrians would see inhabitants of all the lower villages, carrying bundles of their household possessions, clambering with the agility of goats to the almost inaccessible caves near the peaks. A unit of Assyrian mountaineers would be sent off in pursuit, in the hope of catching the local chieftain, but he would have a good start and all the advantages of local knowledge. In the villages little that was portable would have been left behind, so little would remain for the troops to loot. But in a hut here and there fire might still be burning on the hearth, and the soldiers, making torches of brushwood, would apply them to everything combustible, and soon all the huts of the low-lying villages would be ablaze. The hillsmen would be too busy rebuilding

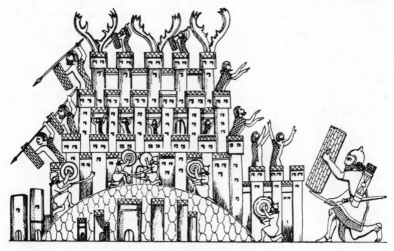

57 A besieged city on fire

their villages to give further trouble with raids on the valley people for a year or two.

The whole campaign might well consist of repeated incidents of this kind, extending over a period of two months or more, since major engagements against foreign armies comparable to the Assyrian army were exceptions rather than the rule. Throughout the campaign Qurdi-Ashur-lamur would generally remain close to the King, acting as a bodyguard in times of danger, as an attendant on formal occasions in camp, and even as a porter when in mountainous territory it was necessary to lift the royal chariot over boulders (58).

58 Carrying the chariot of Sargon II of Assyria

Having seen something of active service, the next year Qurdi-Ashur-lamur might be appointed a junior officer over a cavalry unit with a force sent to reinforce the northern frontier. The immediate reason for such a troop movement would probably be intelligence reports of the mustering of Urartian forces in that area. As a result of minor skirmishing, one or two key mountain villages held by Urartu were perhaps taken, and the Urartian forces dislodged from the area in which they menaced Assyrian security. Subsequently, as winter approached and campaigning became impossible, the main Assyrian force would return to its base, though a few Assyrian officers, of whom we may suppose Qurdi-Ashur-lamur was one, would remain to preserve the *status quo* on the border and to report on any development. During the bitter weather of winter Qurdi-Ashur-lamur might find the population of his villages gradually increasing as some of the original inhabitants, who had fled at the Assyrian approach and had since been living

59 Ashurbanipal hunting
Limestone relief from Kuyunjik, seventh century B.C.

60 A wounded lioness
Limestone relief from Kuyunjik, seventh century B.C.

61 A six-wheeled battering-ram
From the bronze gates of Balawat, ninth century B.C.

out on the mountains, had either to return to their homes and make submission to the Assyrian authorities or stay out on the mountains and probably die of exposure. These peasants would be allowed to go about their business, often proving useful to Qurdi-Ashur-lamur in being the means of bringing intelligence reports about Urartian activities on the other side of the mountain. Such reports would be duly passed back to the capital for evaluation. If they suggested that the Urartians were preparing for a new attack in the spring, a more powerful Assyrian force would be sent to hold the area, freeing Qurdi-Ashur-lamur to return to the capital in time for the New Year Festival in late March (pp. 194–5).

We may imagine, shortly after this, a dispatch rider galloping into the capital with the news that the whole of one sector of the northern frontier was in revolt, the native chieftain who had previously taken an oath of allegiance to Assyria having thrown in his lot with the enemy. The kind of situation which might have occurred was that the chieftain had secretly accepted emissaries from the King of Urartu, who had convinced him that the Urartian forces would shortly drive the Assyrians from the whole area, and had won him over with the promise of exemption from taxation in the future, if he assisted Urartu now. Thus persuaded, the chieftain had led his native levies in a surprise attack upon the local Assyrian garrison. But the Urartian intelligence and communication system was inferior to that of the Assyrians, and if the situation we are imagining followed the usual course the expected Urartian attack might well not have begun until the local revolt had been put down and the rebel leader captured, betrayed by some of his own people to obtain the large reward of gold offered by the Assyrian commander. The unfortunate chieftain would be flayed alive and his skin nailed up prominently on the mountainside as a warning, and some villages which had been active in the revolt burned to the ground. When the expected Urartian attack did come it would be too late, and with the help of contingents sent in by the Assyrian commanders on other sectors of the front, and reinforcements from the homeland, including perhaps Qurdi-Ashur-lamur with his cavalry, it would be easily repulsed.

The revolt and execution of the local native vassal would pose administrative problems to the King and his advisers in the capital. It is likely that the possibility would be considered of appointing a son or brother of the previous chieftain, but, supposing this was not the first occasion upon which the area had given trouble, it would probably be decided, particularly as the area was militarily of some importance, that the time had come to introduce direct rule. The area we are imagining, a group of perhaps a score of villages in an enclave in the mountains, would not be a major appointment, and for general administrative purposes it could be added to the province of a governor with his seat at a major city some thirty miles away. The immediate day-to-day problems of administration and government would, however, make it desirable to have an Assyrian official on the spot. He would be able to keep a watch for any further signs of disloyalty to Assyria, maintain security in the area generally, and, perhaps most important of all, collect and pass on intelligence reports. Much of the military and administrative efficiency of the Assyrian Empire rested ultimately upon an efficient system of communications and intelligence. An Assyrian King, gratefully acknowledging an intelligence report of tribal movements in Babylonia, says: 'The man who loves the house of his lords, opens the ears of his lords to whatever he sees or hears. It is good that you have sent a message and opened my ears.'

We will suppose that for the appointment in question the name of Qurdi-Ashur-lamur was suggested. It was acceptable to the King, but it was also necessary that it should receive the approval of the gods. On a propitious day, therefore, a ceremony was performed in which the will of the Sun-god in the matter was ascertained. A tablet was inscribed, bearing the name of Qurdi-Ashur-lamur, together with the question, 'As to the man whose name is inscribed here, shall he be appointed to such-and-such an appointment?'. This was placed before the symbol of the Sun-god, whilst the divination priests carefully selected a lamb without blemish. This they slaughtered, and having torn out its liver and lungs, by cross-reference to clay models of these organs (36) they made an inventory of favourable and unfavourable signs. The first count gave a clear majority for 'yes!', though had the result been unfavourable there would have been the possibility of taking a second or even a third set of readings.

As *rab alani* (Chief of the Towns) of his area, Qurdi-Ashur-lamur would be in constant touch by messenger not only with his provincial governor but also with the capital. There would be a track leading to the city of the provincial governor, whilst between the governor's city and the plains there were permanent posts where mules were always kept in readiness for messengers carrying dispatches to or from the capital. From the edge of the lowlands a road led direct to the capital.

Qurdi-Ashur-lamur would be responsible not only for the military and political security of his area, but also for the collection of taxes, which were mainly in kind. For assistance he would have a staff which included a scribe serving as Tax Inspector, recording ownership or tenancy of land, noting the state of the rainfall and whether a good or a poor harvest was to be expected, and assessing each farmer's land for the amount of grain due as tax. When the taxes had been assessed and collected, transport still had to be arranged to move the produce to the provincial capital, where it was either stored for use by the army when on operations in that region, or transmitted to the central cities of Assyria. Each village in the area was also responsible for producing every year a certain number of cattle, sheep, and horses, which were sent in large herds to Assyria. Some of the young men probably went with the horses, since the area in which we have imagined Qurdi-Ashur-lamur had a reputation for producing skilled horsemen, and these wild mountaineers would find, not unwillingly, an outlet for their fighting spirit in cavalry contingents in the service of the Assyrian King.

These tax deliveries, like taxes always, were a source of irritation to the natives, and unskilful administration or the propaganda of agents of Urartu from over the border might on occasions lead the local people either to run away into the mountains or to engage in active rebellion. But firm direct Assyrian administration was not all loss. Taxation was an inevitable evil, and whether the villagers were ruled by people of their own or another race made little difference in this respect: if anything, Assyrian taxation probably bore less heavily, since the central administration kept a firm hand on its provincial officials, who were thereby much less likely to be able to extort sums for their own pocket above those required by the Government. Moreover the area had much greater security under Assyrian rule, as Qurdi-Ashur-lamur would be expected by the central government to take stern measures against any attempts by the inhabitants of one mountain village to raid another. If the harvest failed altogether, as it well might in a mountainous area, Qurdi-Ashur-lamur would call upon the provincial capital for an issue of the grain stored there. Probably the villagers had to repay the grain with heavy interest when next they had a good harvest, but meanwhile they were not faced with the sight of their children dying from famine, as had been the situation in

62 The deportation of captives

earlier years. Qurdi-Ashur-lamur also attempted to safeguard the
harvests by damming some of the local mountain streams and
introducing a system of irrigation. However, though this now
became possible as a result of the security given by Assyrian
administration, the idea was not new to the area, and in some of
the more settled mountainous areas over the border the Urartian
authorities were undertaking similar measures.

It frequently happened that when a stable situation had been
secured on Assyria's north-eastern frontier, trouble would break
out in the western part of the Empire, over by the Mediterranean
coast. We may imagine such a situation at this time. In consequence of this a general mobilisation would be proclaimed, Qurdi-
Ashur-lamur, like many other officers in his position, being
required to leave his area in the charge of a subordinate, with a
limited holding force, and to proceed with his own squadron of
cavalry, and as many native levies as he could raise, to the capital
without delay. There he would find assembled a great army, of
something like 200,000 men, prepared to move off for action in
Syria.

The Assyrian army would duly carry out its operations, and
crush the trouble in Syria. Since an account of an actual engagement of the Assyrian army is given later in this chapter, no more
details are necessary here. At the conclusion of the operation, as a
safeguard against further trouble, the Assyrian authorities would
take away from some of the most troublesome cities their leading
citizens and craftsmen and their families, settling them in other

63 Captives resting in transit

parts of the Empire and filling their places in the Syrian cities with corresponding groups from elsewhere (62–3). This policy of transportation was widely used in the Assyrian Empire to deal with troublesome ethnic groups, and has, of course, been employed in the same way in the Soviet Union since the Second World War.

In the major towns of the subdued area the Assyrian authorities would leave administrators, supported by substantial forces, to control local policy. Amongst these administrators we may imagine Qurdi-Ashur-lamur, installed in a town at the foot of the Lebanon range. The local way of life was based, and had been for well over a thousand years, upon felling the cedars in the mountains and preparing the lumber for sending either by ship to Egypt or overland and by river to Assyria and Babylonia. The lumber destined for Egypt was brought down to the wharves ready for loading, as it had always been, but now Qurdi-Ashur-lamur ordered his Tax Inspector to go along to make the necessary assessments for a tax upon this trade. This proved a highly unpopular move with the natives. It was so unpopular that, despite the armed escort accompanying the Tax Inspector, a mob caught him and killed him. This was a dangerous precedent, and Qurdi-Ashur-lamur took immediate action. He sent a message to the nearest garrison for a contingent of troops from a certain tribe, which were often used for police duties in cities. These came into the town and proceeded to knock a little law and order into the rioters. Qurdi-Ashur-lamur then issued a decree that in future all trade with Egypt would be controlled, and that the lumber could only be dispatched under the supervision of the Assyrian authorities.

It is hoped that enough has been said to give some idea of how the imperial administration of Assyria worked. As to Qurdi-Ashur-lamur himself, if he had made a good impression in his early administrative posts he might subsequently rise to a provincial governorship. Of these there were about thirty senior posts, and a varying number of nominal governorships which were not of sufficient importance to entitle the holder to the supreme privilege of officiating at the New Year Festival.

Very little has been said about Qurdi-Ashur-lamur's personal life. Some royal officials amongst the Assyrians were eunuchs, but assuming that Quardi-Ashur-lamur escaped this fate he probably married in his early teens, the marriage arrangements being made between his parents and the parents of the bride. The girl would probably live in his father's household, where he would visit her on his absences from Court, until he was sufficiently senior to set up a household of his own or until his father died and he himself was granted the estate by the King. In the course of his war service Qurdi-Ashur-lamur would be likely from time to time to find among native captives a young lady who took his eye, and there was nothing to prevent him from taking her home as a concubine for himself and a slave-girl for his wife.

64 Two Babylonian ladies

ASSYRIAN WARFARE

Assyria, it is sometimes said, was a State organised primarily for war. This is not the whole truth, but certainly warfare is one of the aspects of Assyrian life upon which we are best informed, particularly during the century of the Sargonid period (722–626 B.C.).

At this period it seems to have been a religious

duty for the King to undertake at least a nominal campaign almost every year. By no means every campaign called out the whole potential military might of the Assyrian Empire; often campaigns were little more than demonstrations against possible trouble-makers, or even mere training manœuvres, and these could be adequately dealt with by the standing army.

The primary reason for the existence of a standing army in Assyria was to safeguard the King against rebellion by his own provincial governors, who might become very powerful men indeed. Within the standing army there were special units who served specifically as bodyguards to the King; these are often described by the King as 'the troops who in a place hostile or friendly never leave my feet'. There were other special permanent units not attached directly to the King, but scattered about the Empire under military officers, and available for immediate action at any trouble point. Some of these were cavalry squadrons of a hundred cavalrymen, like those we have imagined attached to Quardi-Ashur-lamur in his first appointment; others were permanent garrisons in border outposts. Such troops need not have been native Assyrians (and indeed in some cases it can be proved that they were not), but their loyalty to Assyria, and their courage, were probably as unquestionable as the loyalty and courage of the Gurkhas and Sikhs in the forces of British India before 1947.

In times of national emergency the standing army was reinforced by troops raised by provincial governors throughout the Empire. These provincial forces were largely local levies. We may refer to the whole army so constituted as the grand army. There is a good deal of difference of opinion as to the numbers concerned in ancient armies, but the facts seem to indicate that this grand army might run into hundreds of thousands. The kind of evidence upon which this conclusion is based is that in one major action against Elam, enemy casualties are given as 150,000, and in other cases prisoners are numbered in hundreds of thousands.

In many parts of the ancient world military campaigning was a seasonal activity, taking place quite regularly, almost as a summer vacation, between the end of harvest and the resumption of agricultural operations in early winter. In the Bible, for instance, in connection with King David, a season is actually identified as 'the time when kings go forth to battle' (2 Samuel xi 1). At one time this must have been the situation in Assyria also, but this was no longer the case in the Sargonid period. At that period the army might be on campaign at any time of the year, and there was always a striking force ready for immediate action.

The Assyrian army, like every other, marched on its stomach, and part of the credit for its undoubted efficiency must go to the Commissariat. Normally the army took with it basic rations of corn and oil for the troops, and, in areas of operation (such as South Babylonia) where there was likely to be no good grazing, straw or hay for the horses. Corn must have been provided for the horses in any case, since the effectiveness of the cavalry and chariotry depended upon keeping the horses in top condition. Normally the supplies for the troops were distributed as daily rations, but occasionally when the capture of an enemy granary town produced a temporary glut the King could allow the troops to help themselves. When the army passed through an Assyrian province it was the responsibility of the local Assyrian governor to provide for the feeding of the army, and of course elsewhere the army would live off the country as far as possible.

The Assyrian army in its formal order of march must have presented an imposing sight. First came the standards of the gods, apparently wooden or metal symbols on poles, accompanied by

65 Ashurnasirpal crossing a river

the diviners and other religious functionaries. Then came the King in a chariot, surrounded by a bodyguard of young noblemen on foot, and a force of cavalry. On both wings were forces of light infantry, ready to fan out as scouts or snipers if the nature of the country so required. Also attached to the force centred on the King were his staff officers, as well as intelligence officers, interpreters and scribes.

66 A battering-ram

Behind this force came the main army, composed principally of tribal levies, each levy under the command of a provincial governor or one of his staff. The equipment of these levies varied according to the region from which they came, some being slingers, others archers, others cavalrymen, all in their distinctive national dress.

Following the levies came the transport, presumably accompanied and controlled by the engineers. The tasks which confronted the engineers were varied: their duties included the building of bridges across streams, or alternatively the provision of ferry boats (65), the cutting of roads through mountains, the destruction of enemy fortifications, and the building of ramps for use in siege warfare. These ramps consisted of frames of timber with a filling of earth and stones, and their main purpose was to enable battering-rams to be brought into operation against the higher and weaker section of city walls. The battering-rams mentioned are amongst the instruments of war most commonly seen on Assyrian bas-reliefs (61, 66). Basically they consisted of a metal (or metal-clad) pole at the front of an armoured wheeled vehicle. The armoured vehicle gave protection to several men inside who provided the motive power and worked the ram, which in at least some designs of the machine was suspended by chains and could be swung back and forth to increase its momentum and to give a

117

non-stop pounding on the walls. Such machines, together with the other war equipment and the sacks of grain as rations, must have required a considerable body of transport, in the form of wagons and pack-asses, bringing up the rear.

It should be noticed that, contrary to what one might suppose from the writings of some modern authors, Assyrian military campaigns were not a mere succession of massacres and tortures. In general, a newly conquered city or State was not harshly treated, and in many cases its native ruler was left in charge as a vassal, subject to the payment of tribute, the maintenance of a friendly attitude to Assyria, and the installation of an Assyrian representative at the Court. Such a ruler was often made to enter into a formal treaty with Assyria, and Assyrian kings went into considerable administrative detail in such treaties with their vassals, as to what they might or might not do. Thus in a treaty with the King of Tyre, Esarhaddon says: 'You shall not open a letter that I send you without the *Qipu*-official [the Assyrian representative]. If the *Qipu*-official is not at hand, you shall await him (and then) open (it).' It was only when such a vassal broke his oath of allegiance that he and his country were likely to be treated with severity; but even in such cases it was only the leaders of the city or State who were likely to be tortured or mutilated. Death or mutilation was not the invariable fate awaiting those who had rebelled against Assyria. Of one city Esarhaddon relates: 'I cast their king Asukhili into fetters and brought (him) to Assyria. I made him sit tied up near the gate of the inner city of Nineveh with a bear, a dog, and a pig.' Generally the worst that was likely to happen to the mass of the people, and then only when they had repeatedly shown themselves troublesome, was that they were deported to another part of the Assyrian Empire, as in the well-known instance of the Israelites at the capture of Samaria. Of course, it may be said that the Assyrians were blameworthy for the mere fact of being imperialists, but imperialism is not necessarily wrong: there are circumstances in which it may be both morally right and necessary. Such was the case in the Near East in the early first millennium. But for the Assyrian Empire the whole of the achievements of the previous 2000 years of civilization might have been lost in anarchy, as a host of tiny kingdoms (like Israel, Judah, and Moab) played at war amongst themselves, or it might have been swamped under hordes of the savage peoples who were constantly attempting to push southwards from beyond the Caucasus.

67 The siege of a city

It may be of some interest to give such details as we have of one particular Assyrian engagement. The example chosen was not a punitive expedition against troublesome vassals, but an attack upon a dangerous coalition headed by Assyria's northern neighbour Urartu (in the region later known as Armenia).

In the summer of 714 B.C. King Sargon set off to the region east and north of Assyria with the object (as he put it) of 'muzzling the mouth of the insolent, binding the halter upon the over-bold'. In plain language, he intended to deal with the threat that the two growing kingdoms of Zikirtu (an Iranian people) and Urartu (a people related at some distance to the Hurrians) constituted to Assyria's security and its control of the trade routes running from Iran and beyond to the west. After certain minor operations amongst his vassals and tributaries in the eastern mountains, Sargon made contact with the King of Zikirtu, who withdrew his main force to link up with the King of Urartu, leaving small forces in mountain outposts to harass Sargon in his pursuit. The terrain was difficult, and by the time Sargon had reached the area held by Ursa, King of Urartu, his forces were in bad morale, and he no longer had full tactical control of his whole army. He frankly says:

> I could not give ease to their weariness, I could not give them water to drink, I could not set up the camp and I could not fix the defence of the headquarters. I could not direct my advance-guards (with the result that) I could not gather them in to me; my units of the right and left had not returned to my side; and I could not await the rear-guard.

Ursa of Urartu and Metatti of Zikirtu drew up their battle line in a defile of the mountain in difficult terrain and awaited the coming of Sargon. No doubt they had foreseeen that the nature of the country would cause Sargon difficulty in maintaining tactical control over the whole of his forces. Actually, although the place in question, a defile in the mountain, doubtless seemed to Ursa an excellent place in which to catch and mop up the Assyrian army, it was in fact an extremely grave tactical error on his part to engage his whole army in a defensive battle in such circumstances. The great German strategist and tactician von Clausewitz goes to great length in his book *On War* to point out that though small bodies of troops may offer powerful resistance in mountainous country, it is tactical folly to commit a whole army to a defensive action in such territory.

Sargon appears to have recognised that Ursa's tactical error had placed a major victory within his grasp, in circumstances which fully outweighed his own breakdown of communications. Therefore, although most of his army was not immediately available for action, he made an attack at once. His attack was headed by his personal squadron of cavalry, although Sargon himself, presumably for ceremonial reasons, was in a light

68 A vulture finds a meal
(Detail of battlefield scene)

chariot. The cavalry, consisting of mounted archers and lancers, cut straight into the centre of the opposing forces, shooting down the enemy chariot horses, and making straight for Ursa's headquarters. The faulty tactics of Ursa had deprived his chariotry of the possibility of manœuvre, and the cavalry onslaught caused havoc. Most of Ursa's staff officers and cavalry were compelled to surrender, though Ursa himself managed to slip away on a mare, to the derision of the Assyrians, who held that if a King rode a horse at all it should be a stallion. The surrender of the Urartian cavalry underlines the bad generalship of Ursa. Sargon specifically says that the Urartian army had the best-trained horses in the world. His actual statement, with reference to a particular region of Urartu, goes as follows:

As to the people who live in that area in the land of Urartu, . . . their

69 An Assyrian battlefield

70 Breaking a wild horse

like does not exist for skill with cavalry horses. The foals, young steeds born in the King's spacious land, which they rear for his royal contingents and catch yearly, until they are taken to the land of Subi and their quality becomes apparent, will never have had anyone straddling their backs; yet in advancing, wheeling, retreating, or battle disposition, they are never seen to break out of control.

With the Urartian army completely demoralised and defeated, Sargon now turned to Zikirtu. Here there was a different formation and this required different tactics. The forces of Zikirtu were organised not as a national army but on a tribal or territorial basis. Sargon's tactics here were to break up the battle formation by separating the tributaries from their overlord (the King of Zikirtu) and then to smash up the disorganised units.

The defeat of the Zikirtian and Urartian armies need not have meant the final defeat of Urartu, for, as von Clausewitz points out, at such a stage the conqueror is now at the same disadvantage at which the defender stood before. If the defenders take up arms in a determined guerilla action in the mountains, the attacker can still be defeated.

Here, however, the psychological aspects of Assyrian warfare had their effect. Sargon was deep in hostile territory and might well have been exposed to crippling guerilla warfare. That he was not was in part the consequence of his own use of propaganda. The Assyrian kings frequently mention that they poured out terror upon the enemy land, and this represented not—as has often been suggested—an act of sadism, but the employment of terrorism for the purposes of psychological warfare. In the absence of mass media of communications, the only means of softening up an enemy population in advance of the army was by the use of terror, spreading from village to village and town to town with reports of the ferocity of the Assyrian forces. It was this kind of thing which protected the Assyrian army from guerilla warfare after its victory over the main armies of Urartu and Zikirtu. Sargon specifically mentions that after he had inflicted that defeat, 'the rest of the people, who had fled to save their lives, I let go free to glorify the victory of the god Ashur my lord'. Some of these poor wretches died from exposure in the mountains, but others reached home, where their terrifying account of the devastating striking power of the Assyrian forces had the required effect. Sargon goes on to record: 'Their leaders, men who understood battle and who had fled before my weapons, drew near to them covered with the venom of death, and recounted to them the glory of Ashur, . . . so that they became like dead men.' The methods of Assyrian psychological warfare may be distasteful to us in modern times, but one need go no further than this comment of Sargon to see that it had a high military value, and did not spring from some sadistic element peculiar to the Assyrian character.

Chapter VI

ANCIENT CRAFTS AND INDUSTRIES

IN the third century B.C., when Babylonian civilisation was, except for a few priests and astronomers, virtually dead, a Babylonian priest named Berossus wrote an account of the traditions of his people. This account, written not in Sumerian or Akkadian but in Greek, included a description of the supposed origin of civilisation. According to Berossus,

> In the first year [of the world] there appeared, from the Persian Gulf, a being named Oannes. His whole body was that of a fish. Under the fish's head he had another head, and joined to the fish's tail were feet like those of a man. . . . This being used to pass the day among men, and gave them knowledge of written documents and all kinds of knowledge and crafts. He taught them to construct cities, to found temples, to compile laws, and to survey the land; and made known to them the use of seeds and the gathering of fruit. In short, he instructed them in everything necessary for daily life. From that time nothing further has been discovered.

Two thousand years before this there had been a Sumerian myth in circulation, describing how the Water-god Enki (also the god of Wisdom) had created the world order. This god had created the sheepfolds, instituted cattle rearing, and given to the world such things as irrigation, fishing, ploughing and cultivation, the use of grain, brick-making and metal-working, and women's crafts such as spinning and weaving.

Despite the gap of two millennia, the underlying idea is clearly the same. It was recognised that civilisation was in the first place based upon certain early developments in man's mastery of his environment and available materials, of such a fundamental nature that they could be considered the revelation of a god. Put more bluntly, the people of Babylonia, from first to last, took the view (whether rightly or wrongly) that what lay at the basis of civilisation was not simply spiritual values, but included a considerable measure of what we might now call technology.

124

We notice that Berossus, looking back from a period when Babylonian civilisation had only a past and no future, believed that since the original revelation by Oannes nothing further had been discovered. His predecessors of 2000 years before had known better.

The more ancient myth concerning Enki and the world order seems primarily to describe the state of human achievement at the time of the coming of the Sumerians into Mesopotamia. The

71 Enki, god of Wisdom

Sumerians did not of course suddenly appear and create civilisation out of nothing, and many cultural advances had taken place in the Near East (not necessarily in Mesopotamia) before the Sumerians ever arrived on the scene. Most of these early advances in the Near East were of a kind as fundamental to our own civilisation as to the Sumerian way of life. Our principal food animals, the sheep and the ox, were domesticated there, and barley and wheat were first cultivated in the same area. It was in some part of the Near East, possibly Mesopotamia itself, that large-scale irrigation and the use of the ox-drawn plough first began. Pottery and metal technology both had their origin not far from Mesopotamia. Spinning and weaving, widely known in prehistoric times, were also crafts practised in pre-Sumerian Mesopotamia. Though all these developments were known before the coming of the Sumerians, it was the Sumerians who were the first people to be acquainted with all of them at once. Ever afterwards life was unthinkable for them (as indeed it would be for us) without these material foundations. It was all these achievements, existing before the Sumerians reached Mesopotamia, which they thought of as the basis of the world order established by Enki.

The earliest Sumerians did not, however, passively accept the world order as unchangeable in all its details, and they added their

72 Copper lion's head, *c.* 2900 B.C.

own inventions and discoveries to the prehistoric legacy which had come down to them. Some such technological advances we have to infer from archaeological sources, though one or two are reflected in Sumerian myths. There is, for example, a myth referring to the beginning of shade-tree gardening, that is, the planting of trees to give vegetables some protection against the scorching sun of Mesopotamia and to reduce soil erosion.

We know something of the details of Sumerian agriculture in the third millennium B.C. from an ancient Sumerian text, one of many which have been pieced together by the noted Sumerologist S. N. Kramer of Philadelphia. The text gives instructions in the form of advice from a father to a son. The following account is based on Professor Kramer's latest discussion and translation of the composition in his book *The Sumerians* (Chicago, 1963).

When a man started work in his field, he had first to irrigate it, but must ensure that the water did not rise too high. After the water had been run off, oxen, wearing some kind of shoe, were driven over the field to tread down the weeds. These oxen, trampling about in the mud, would leave the surface very uneven, and it therefore needed to be worked over and levelled by men with mattocks, and afterwards by a drag, presumably some kind of harrow.

The field next had to be ploughed, with two different types of plough, and then harrowed and raked. Finally any clods that still remained were broken up with hammers. All this obviously required a substantial labour force and hard work all round, and the farmer in our text is advised to keep a constant watch on his men. This part of the operations was expected to occupy a full ten days, continuing by starlight as well as during the daytime.

The field was now ready for sowing. This was done by means of a seeder plough, an implement with a vertical funnel above the ploughshare, so arranged that seed could be dropped straight into the bottom of the furrow (*37*). A man with a bag of barley walked

73 Ploughing

alongside this plough and was expected to drop the seed in at a uniform rate and to make sure that it went to a depth of about an inch and a half. When the sowing had been done, the field was once again levelled and any remaining clods broken up.

As soon as the barley began to sprout, the farmer had to say a prayer to the goddess of Vermin, and to take his own measures by scaring off the birds. Amongst the worst of the ancient farmer's possible troubles at this stage, though the Sumerian text does not mention them, were locust swarms. As the crop grew, it had to be irrigated three times, at stages which are carefully defined in terms of the height of the barley. The third irrigation was when the barley was at its full height. This was a time of some anxiety, and the farmer had to keep a careful watch for any sign of the fungus disease we generally call 'rust', which is marked by a reddening of the affected plant. If the farmer got past this danger successfully, he could now give a fourth irrigation, which, it was estimated, would increase the final yield by ten per cent.

There were equally detailed instructions for the harvesting. This was to be done as soon as the barley was fully ripe: it was not to be left until some of it started to droop. The harvesting team consisted of three men. There was a reaper, a second man to bind the sheaves, and a third man to set up the sheaves in stooks. Gleaners were allowed in the field to pick up fallen ears of barley, but were not, of course, allowed to interfere with the sheaves.

The threshing and winnowing now followed, taking place at a special threshing floor. According to Professor Kramer the threshing was in two stages, mounds of barley first being run over by wagons for five days and the grain then extracted from the ears by the use of a special threshing sledge. But there would seem to be no obvious point in the first part of the operation. It is therefore suggested that this part of the text simply means that wagon loads of barley were standing by, and would be driven up to be unloaded on the threshing floor as soon as required.

In any case, it is quite clear that the actual threshing was done with a threshing sledge. This consisted of a wooden frame with teeth of stones or metal bedded into bitumen underneath and secured with leather thongs. Oxen dragged this instrument round and round over the ears of corn, with the driver sitting on the sledge to increase the pressure. The same method of threshing could still be seen in use around Jerusalem as recently as 1947.

The final operation, the winnowing, was carried out by two men described as 'barley-lifters'. The method of separation was apparently to throw the mixture of grain, chaff and dust into the air when a strong wind was blowing. The light rubbish would be carried away, leaving a heap of clean grain.

In the text summarised above the reference was throughout to barley. It has been mentioned that wheat was known in Mesopotamia in pre-Sumerian times, and throughout Mesopotamian history it has usually been grown to some extent. However, it was always grown less than barley, and in third-millennium Sumer, as the botanist Hans Helbaek has pointed out, barley seems to have been grown almost to the exclusion of wheat from about 2700 B.C. This was probably a consequence of irrigation. Helbaek points out that repeated irrigation gradually increases the salinity of the soil, and since wheat is less tolerant of salinity than barley, the land would become unusable for wheat sooner than for barley. Ultimately the barley crops would also fail, and this may explain why some of the early Sumerian settlements ceased to be inhabited.

The third important crop in ancient Mesopotamia was sesame, grown as a source of oil: the name of this plant in both Sumerian and Akkadian means 'oil plant'. Amongst other agricultural products were, as mentioned elsewhere, dates and various vegetables.

Animal husbandry was also of considerable importance in the economy of the Sumerians from earliest times. Both oxen and small cattle (that is, sheep and goats) were bred from the beginning of the historical period, but the small cattle were always by far the more numerous, many different breeds being known. From the period of the Third Dynasty of Ur (around 2100 B.C.) we have records of flocks of sheep running into tens of thousands. It has been shown that at this time male sheep were castrated on a considerable scale, though the practice largely went out of use in the succeeding Old Babylonian period.

The sheep and goats were, of course, valuable not only as a source of food and as sacrificial animals for the temples (74), but also for their wool and hair. The original way of collecting sheep's wool was to pluck it, a method which shearing had not wholly superseded by 1400 B.C.

Professor Th. Jacobsen of Harvard has given an interesting account of the textile industry just before 2000 B.C., his evidence coming from an archive found near the temple of Nanna at Ur. This archive dealt with the economic interests of the King, in particular those related to the wool and textile industry.

74 Sumerian carrying lamb as offering

The herdsmen in charge of the royal flocks paid their wool into the central depot, where there were separate stores for the wool from fat-tailed sheep, from flocks of other breeds, and also for hair from goats. At the end of each year all stocks were taken out into the open for stock-taking, and incidentally, one may suppose, for an airing.

Issues of wool were made from time to time. Some of these were for cult purposes (for equipment for the gods, and so on), whilst other issues were made to male and female slaves and other workers in the service of the King. The figures for these issues have permitted the incidental calculation that at this time the number of slaves in the service of the King was about 9000.

The wool went out from the stores to be spun and woven in the villages and towns around Ur. Spinning and weaving were originally predominantly female occupations, and were still so at this time. The cloth produced by the weavers then went to fullers who treated it in an alkaline solution made from the ashes of a particular plant. The wool might then be dyed with various dyes of vegetable origin, or, in the case of the most valuable cloth, with the famous purple from shell-fish collected on the coast of Syria.

The woollen cloth produced covered a wide range of quality, from that fit for a King to that only suitable for a slave. In addition to woollen cloth, linen was also produced, though on a smaller scale, and flax (the raw material for linen) is mentioned in the archive we have referred to.

Another material extensively used in the ancient—as in the modern—world, was leather, and there is frequent mention of leather-workers. Needless to say, the usual source was the hides of cows or oxen and the skins of sheep and goats. Pig skins were also used. The skins were tanned by steeping them in a solution of alum together with an infusion made from gall-nuts (oak-apples); both alum and gall-nuts had to be imported from the north and at all times were important items of commerce. Amongst the things for which leather was used were items of clothing, shoes and sandals, shields and helmets, horse harness, slings, the tyres of chariots, coverings for chairs and chariots, bags and various kinds of container, skins for holding liquids, and membranes for drums.

One of the most important aspects of ancient Mesopotamian industry was its metal technology, though Mesopotamia played no part in the earliest stage of metal utilisation.

Copper ores are of widespread occurrence in the mountains north of Mesopotamia, from Anatolia to the Caspian Sea, and the archaeological evidence indicates that it was somewhere in this region, most probably in Iran just after 4000 B.C., that true copper technology began. By 'true copper technology' we mean first the melting and casting of copper occurring as a pure metal and then the smelting of copper ores. The details of these developments go well outside the period and area with which this book deals, but it may be mentioned that the old theory that copper was first smelted from its ores accidentally over a camp fire is now generally discounted, as the necessary temperature would scarcely be achieved. It is more probable that the process of smelting copper ores was first discovered in furnaces of the type used for making pottery. In such furnaces, used in northern Mesopotamia and Iran by 4000 B.C., temperatures of up to 1200°C could be achieved, and this was easily sufficient not only to smelt copper from its ores (requiring a temperature of 700°–800°C) but also to melt the pure metal (melting point 1085°C). Metallic copper often occurs naturally in association with its ores, which are in the form of blue stones, and an early metallurgist might well put a mixed lump of this kind into a furnace with the object of melting the copper away from the stone. If the man found that he ended with much more copper than he had started with, and that most of the stone had disappeared, he would rightly conclude that he could 'cook' copper out of that sort of blue stone. This may well have been the way in which the process of copper smelting was discovered.

The smelting of copper certainly did not begin in Mesopotamia, but the use of the metal (extremely limited at first) soon spread into the area. By about 2900 B.C. it was in relatively common use, being employed for such things as vases, bowls, mirrors, cosmetic pots, fish-hooks, chisels, daggers, hoes and axes(75).

It was shortly after this time that, so far as Mesopotamia is concerned, the general use of bronze began. Bronze is an alloy of copper and tin, and has the advantage of being both harder than pure copper and easier to cast. Its production may be achieved either by smelting a mixture of copper ores and tin ores, or by melting together pure copper and pure tin. The very variable composition of early bronze suggests that the alloy was first produced from the mixed ores, only later being made by mixing metallic copper and tin. Several objects of bronze, such as vases, swords and axes, occur in the celebrated Royal Tombs of Ur, now generally dated at about 2600 B.C. One of the finest ancient examples of ancient metal-work is a bronze head, generally supposed to be that of Sargon of Agade (c. 2350 B.C.), now in the Iraq Museum (13).

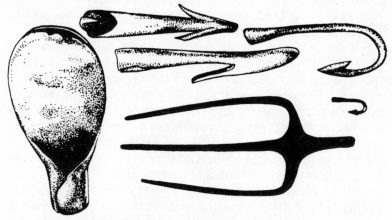

75 Tools: bronze fish-trident, fish-hooks and hoe

The copper ore used by the people of South Mesopotamia in the third millennium came either overland from somewhere in Iran, or by sea up the Persian Gulf from countries called Magan and Melukhkha, which have not yet been identified, despite endless discussion. The analyses of copper and bronze objects of this period show that in Sumerian times it was the surface ores which were used and not the deeper lying ones (which occur as sulphides); thus no deep mining was involved. We have some idea of the appearance of the furnaces in which the ore was smelted, since not only have remains of furnaces been found, but also one of the Sumerian ideograms meaning 'furnace' is found in a very early form as a recognisable picture of a furnace:

The fuel used for such a furnace was wood and bundles of reeds. The smiths had bellows available to increase the draught and raise the temperature.

The copper produced by smelting would be very impure and would require further treatment to make it usable for the production of bronze or for casting as pure copper. This second operation was probably performed in a different and smaller type of furnace, but we have no direct evidence about this. There are, however, Egyptian pictures of metal-workers using a blowpipe on a crucible in a small furnace, and these probably represent the final purifying of crude copper before casting. The technique used in Mesopotamia may have been similar.

For the casting of copper or bronze, there were three methods which might be used. In order of development, these were the open-mould, the closed-mould, and the *cire perdue* (or lost-wax) methods. The open-mould and the closed-mould methods are self-explanatory, but the *cire perdue* method may need a brief description. Basically it was as follows. A core was made of clay or sand and given a coating of wax, of which the outer surface was shaped into the required form. A coating of clay was then put over the wax, leaving holes at top and bottom. If necessary it could be arranged for wires to run from the inner core to the outer clay coating to keep them in position relative to each other. When the clay was dry the whole arrangement was embedded in sand and heated. The wax ran out of the bottom and molten metal was poured into the space the wax had previously occupied. When the metal had cooled the outer coating of clay and the inner core were chipped away.

Other techniques of metal-working already in use in the first half of the third millennium B.C. included riveting, soldering, hammering and annealing, and, in the case of precious metals, filigree work and granulation.

Iron was not used to any extent in Mesopotamia (or elsewhere in the Near East) until much later, though a few specimens, in the form of beads and amulets, do occur from 3000 B.C. onwards. Most of these examples of iron were of meteoric origin, though there are a few examples of man-made iron from the third millennium B.C. One may ask why, if iron could be made in the third millennium B.C., it was not used. The fact was that there was no inducement to use it, except for ornaments, as not only was it more difficult to work than bronze but it was also (with the techniques then available) less strong. The situation did not change markedly until after 1500 B.C., when it was discovered, presumably in the Hittite region, that iron could be made extremely hard by the process which we know as carburising, which at that time could be achieved by keeping iron in a fire of glowing charcoal for a long period. This new technique gradually spread throughout the Near East and came into use in Mesopotamia from about 1300 B.C.

Throughout the 2500 years of ancient Mesopotamian history there were large numbers of other crafts and industries, but there is space only to mention a few of the most important. There was the basket-maker, who exercised a craft going back to prehistoric times, and wove his products out of reeds, palm leaves, and similar materials. It was probably he who made the part of the bed which a Babylonian actually lay on, as the terracotta models of beds indicate that this was of matting of some kind (76). The person who made the frame of the bed was of course the carpenter. He also produced such things as chairs and tables, doors for houses, boats, wagons and chariots, cages for animals, the wooden parts of ploughs, chests

76 A bed

133

77 Assyrian craftsmen

and boxes, and a host of other things. His principal tools were the hammer, chisel, saw, and later the bow drill. The hard woods needed by the carpenter had to be obtained, either by trade or by military expedition, from the Persian highlands or the Lebanon, since the only timber available in Babylonia was palm, willow and Euphrates poplar, none of which are of use for any but the crudest work, though they were good for fuel either as cut, or converted into charcoal.

Another very ancient craft was that of the potter, to whom we possibly owe the invention of the wheel, which we find first employed for making pottery shortly after 3500 B.C. The potter was a craftsman whose status was adversely affected by the developments which took place around 3000 B.C. Before that, the products of the potter had been finely decorated, so that some of the examples which remain have considerable aesthetic appeal to most people even today (78). Unfortunately for the potter's art, with the technological developments associated with the early Sumerians the situation arose that all really fine vessels were made of metal or stone, and the ware of the potter came to be considered as purely utilitarian and no longer worthy of fine decoration. None the less, the forms of the products of the Babylonian or Assyrian potter are often of considerable elegance (79, 84).

Other crafts to which a passing reference may be made were those of the sculptors. There were sculptors who produced work in ivory or wood and others who worked in stone. We have no direct evidence that they formed two distinct groups, but the techniques must have been so different that it is a reasonable conclusion that this was so. Their work was always in the main destined to serve as dedications for the temples. There may also be mentioned the gem-cutters who produced amongst other things the cylinder seals so widely used by Sumerian, Babylonian and Assyrian gentlemen.

The crafts mentioned above were a few amongst many which were known from before 3000 B.C. A craft which developed in Mesopotamia some centuries after the arrival of the Sumerians was that of the glass-maker. Some people, knowing that glazed objects and small glass beads are found in prehistoric Egypt, might be inclined to dispute this claim, but it should be pointed out that no vessels of worked glass are found in Egypt before 1500 B.C. This leads the authorities on this subject to conclude that the Egyptians learnt the craft of glass-working from Mesopotamia, where pieces of well-made glass are found as early as the middle of the third millennium B.C.

78 Babylonian vase, *c.* 2100 B.C.

A number of cuneiform texts from Mesopotamia are known which give actual recipes for the making of glass or glazes, the earliest of them coming from 1700 B.C., though the advanced stage reflected by the earliest texts shows a long previous tradition of

79 Pottery from Nimrud

135

glass-making. Glass-making was not a hit-or-miss affair, and the Mesopotamian glass-makers knew how to produce different types ànd colours of their products by the addition of various ingredients. Modern technologists have carried out the instructions on the ancient texts and successfully produced glazed vessels by them.

Once glass had been obtained, the actual technique of making vessels from it was to soften glass rods by heat and wind them round a central core of the appropriate shape. The completed vessel would then have its surface consolidated by further heat treatment, when if required patterns could be added(80). The technique of glass-blowing was not invented until the first century B.C.

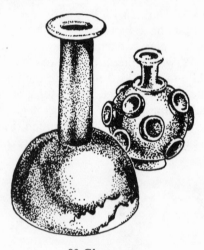

80 Glass-ware

Chapter VII

LAW

IN December 1901 and January 1902 there were found three large pieces of diorite (a black rock), bearing an inscription which revolutionised the current view of the civilisation of the ancient Near East. Those three pieces of stone, discovered by French archaeologists excavating at Susa (in ancient times the capital of Elam in southern Persia), were found to form a single monument. This was the now famous stele bearing the laws of Hammurabi(*82*), datable to just before 1750 B.C. Its presence in Susa must have derived from its having at some time been taken off as booty in an Elamite raid, since its contents show that it was originally made and set up in Babylonia, possibly at Babylon itself, though some scholars argue that it came from Sippar.

The Stele of Hammurabi, now in the Louvre, stands about seven feet six inches high. On the top of the monument is a representation of the Sun-god, who was also the god of Justice, receiving the homage of King Hammurabi. Beneath is engraved the text of the inscription: the writing runs from top to bottom in a number of bands divided horizontally. In the inscription the laws themselves are sandwiched between a prologue and an epilogue. The prologue begins with a claim that the gods called Hammurabi 'to make justice visible in the land, to destroy the wicked person and the evil-doer, that the strong might not injure the weak', and contains a series of titles in which Hammurabi boasts of his piety towards the gods and his care for their cities and shrines. The epilogue speaks of the purpose of the writing down of the laws, which is 'to set right the orphan and widow . . . and wronged person', and goes on to recommend succeeding rulers to pay heed to Hammurabi's words, on pain of incurring the curses of the gods upon whom Hammurabi calls. The laws themselves consisted originally of about 280 sections, of which some thirty-five were erased from the stele in antiquity, presumably by the conqueror who took the monument to Susa. Fortunately, about half the missing text can now be restored, partly from some diorite fragments which must come from another monument of the same kind, and partly from clay tablets of various periods containing parts of Hammurabi's laws.

The publication of these laws stirred up a violent controversy, of which the last ripples are still faintly visible in some Scripture textbooks. Without any doubt these laws had been in existence several centuries before the period at which Moses, the great Hebrew law giver, lived. Also without any doubt, the laws of Hammurabi frequently legislated for the same kind of circumstances, sometimes in almost identical terms, as those laws, supposedly of divine origin, associated with the name of Moses. Direct borrowing seemed indicated. Orthodox theologians, mentally wriggling in embarrassment, sought to point out that, where similarities could not be denied, the Hebrew laws showed a higher ethical content. (In fact, this is not always true.) Opponents of religion gleefully argued that the Hebrew law giver (whether Moses or some later legislator sheltering beneath the venerable name) had simply taken over, in the name of his God, as much of the existing Babylonian law as suited him, adapting it to the more primitive sociology of the Hebrew people. One such writer stated dogmatically: 'if there be any relationship between the Hebrew and the Babylonian legislations [and the rest of the little book makes it clear that the author had no doubts on the matter], there is only one possible conclusion, and that is that the Hebrew was borrowed from the earlier Babylonian'.

Later discoveries and research have shown that, though there are problems in plenty about both the Mosaic law and the laws of Hammurabi, the controversy about the relationship between the two was based upon a misunderstanding. Since the original discovery of the Stele of Hammurabi, there have been found quite a few other collections of laws from the ancient Near East, four of them certainly older than the laws of Hammurabi, and these show beyond any doubt that the existence of written laws, far from being an exceptional circumstance, was a common and probably an essential element of civilised life. Thus the existence of two collections of laws at different times in different places did not necessarily mean that the later was a direct borrowing from the earlier. Furthermore, any similarities in detail might be adequately accounted for by acquaintance with customary legal practice and with the existence of a basically similar social structure, which would give rise to the need for legislation upon similar matters.

LAW

With the earlier controversy no longer relevant, attention has now turned to a different matter, the origin and purpose of the laws of Hammurabi in the form in which we know them. Before this point is discussed, however, it seems advisable to give some account of the contents of the laws themselves.

The arrangement of the laws shows a deliberate attempt at a systematic treatment of the material, laws concerned with similar aspects of life being brought together. Thus the first five sections, containing laws dealing with false accusations, false witness, and corrupt judges, have as their common link the administration of justice. A brief analysis of the whole of the laws may be made as follows:

Administration of justice (5 sections)
Offences against property (20 sections)
Land tenure (about 50 sections)
Trade and commercial transactions (nearly 40 sections)
The family as a social institution (68 sections), covering such matters as adultery, marriage, concubinage, desertion, divorce, incest, adoption, inheritance.
Penalties for assault (20 sections)
Professional services (16 sections), concerning rates of payment for satisfactory, and penalties for unsatisfactory, performance of services.
Draught-oxen (16 sections), dealing with such matters as rates of hire, mishaps to oxen let out on hire, dangerous oxen.
Agriculture and herdsmen (11 sections), including wage rates of labourers and herdsmen, and dishonesty.
Rates of hire of animals, wagons or boats: wages of labourers and craftsmen (10 sections)
Ownership and sale of slaves (5 sections)

It need hardly be pointed out that it can be misleading to quote particular laws without at the same time considering the social situation in which they arose, but with this warning the following are offered as specimens of the laws on the Stele of Hammurabi. The headings are explanatory comments by the present author and not part of the original text.

§§3, 4 *False witness*

If a man has come forward in a lawsuit for the witnessing of false things, and has not proved the thing that he said, if that lawsuit is a capital case, that man shall be put to death. If he came forward for

139

witnessing about corn or silver, he shall bear the penalty (which would apply to) that case.

§16 *Theft by finding*

If a man has concealed in his house a lost slave or slave-girl belonging to the Palace or to a subject, and has not brought him [or her] out at the proclamation of the Crier, the owner of the house shall be put to death. [To those whose attitude to slavery is coloured by memories of *Uncle Tom's Cabin*, it should be emphasised that the man concealing the slave would certainly have had no idea of making a 'direct action' protest against slavery as an institution. He was simply a rogue who hoped, by keeping quiet about his find, to acquire someone else's slave for nothing.]

§25 *Looting*

If a fire has broken out in a man's house, and a man who has gone to extinguish it has cast his eye on the property of the owner of the house and has taken the property of the owner of the house, that man shall be thrown into the fire.

§48 *Moratorium in case of hardship*

If a man is subject to a debt bearing interest, and Adad [the Weather-god] has saturated his field or a high flood has carried (its crop) away, or because of lack of water he has not produced corn in that field, in that year he shall not return any corn to (his) creditor. He shall cancel [literally 'wet'] his tablet, and he shall not pay interest for that year.

§128 *The status 'wife' depends upon a contract*

If a man has taken a wife, but has not set down a contract for her, that woman is not (legally) a wife. [The contract concerned need not have been of a complicated form. One from the period of the Third Dynasty of Ur, over two centuries before Hammurabi, reads as follows: 'Puzur-khaya has taken Ubartum as his wife. The oath by the King has been taken before [four named persons], acting as witnesses. Year in which Enamgalanna was installed as *En*-priest of Inanna.']

§§129, 132 *Adultery*

If a gentleman's wife has been caught lying with another male, they shall tie them up and throw them into the water. If the wife's lord lets his wife live, then the King shall let his servant live.

If there is a gentleman's wife against whom the finger has been pointed on account of another male, but she has not been caught lying with another male, for her husband's sake she shall jump into

81 (*above*) A Cassite boundary-stone
with divine symbols
Probably from Nippur, twelfth century B.C.

82 (*right*) Stele of Hammurabi, King of
Babylon 1792–1750 B.C.

83 A carved ivory
From Nimrud, eighth century B.C.

84 A faience vase
From Ashur, early first millennium B.C.

85 Bull-vaulting in Crete
From a bronze statuette, second millennium B.C.
(Not represented in Mesopotamian art, but possibly referred to in
the *Epic of Gilgamesh*: see p. 87)

the holy river. [This refers not to compulsory suicide, but to establishing the woman's innocence of guilt by the river ordeal. On the river ordeal, see below, p. 154.]

§141 *Treatment of a wastrel wife*

If a gentleman's wife, living in the gentleman's house, has set her mind to go out [this probably means that she sets up a separate house rather than that she goes out on a shopping spree], and spends(?) (their) assets(?), and squanders her household and makes her husband('s estate) small, this shall be proved against her; if her husband then says he will divorce her, he may divorce her and nothing shall be given to her as divorce-money for her journey. If her husband does not say he will divorce her, her husband may marry another woman, and that woman [*i.e.* the original wife] shall remain in her husband's house as a slave-girl.

§§146, 147 *Concubinage*

If a man has married a *Naditu*-priestess, and she has given a slave-girl to her husband and (the slave-girl) has borne children, and afterwards that slave-girl puts herself on a par with her mistress, because she has borne children her mistress may not sell her for silver, but she may put a slave-mark on her and number her with the slave-girls. If she has not borne children, her mistress may sell her for silver.

§153 'The eternal triangle'

If a gentleman's wife has had her husband killed on account of another man, they shall impale that woman on a stake.

§157 *Incest*

If a man after (the death of) his father lies sexually with his mother, they shall burn both of them.

§165 *Inheritance, and the right to bequeath property by will*

If a man has donated field, orchard or house to his favourite heir and has written a sealed document for him (to confirm this), after the father has gone to his doom, when the brothers share he [the favourite heir] shall take the gift that his father gave him, and apart from that they shall share equally in the property of the paternal estate.

§§188, 189 *Adoption and apprenticeship*

If an artisan has taken a child for bringing up, and has taught him his manual skill, (the child) shall not be (re)claimed. If he has not taught him his manual skill, that pupil may return to his father's house.

§§195–99, 205, 206 *Assault*

If a son has struck his father, they shall cut off his hand.

If a man has destroyed the eye of a man of the 'gentleman' class, they shall destroy his eye. If he has broken a gentleman's bone, they shall break his bone. If he has destroyed the eye of a commoner or broken a bone of a commoner, he shall pay one mina of silver. If he has destroyed the eye of a gentleman's slave, or broken a bone of a gentleman's slave, he shall pay half (the slave's) price.

If a gentleman's slave strikes the cheek of a man of the 'gentleman' class, they shall cut off (the slave's) ear.

If a gentleman strikes a gentleman in a free fight and inflicts an injury on him, that man shall swear 'I did not strike him deliberately', and he shall pay the surgeon. [*i.e.* the man's liability is limited to paying the surgeon.]

§§215–18 *Fees and penalties connected with surgery*

If a surgeon has made a serious wound [presumably meaning 'a deep incision'] in a gentleman with a bronze knife, and has thereby saved the gentleman's life, . . . he shall receive ten shekels of silver. If (the patient is) a commoner, he shall receive five shekels of silver. If (the patient is) a gentleman's slave, the slave's master shall pay the surgeon two shekels of silver.

If the surgeon has made a serious wound in a gentleman with a bronze knife, and has thereby caused the gentleman to die, . . . they shall cut off (the surgeon's) hand.

§§229–30 *Treatment of jerry-builders*

If a builder has made a house for a man but has not made his work strong, so that the house he made falls down and causes the death of the owner of the house, that builder shall be put to death. If it causes the death of the son of the owner of the house, they shall kill the son of that builder.

86 Ox, with one horn removed and the other capped to prevent goring

§§250–52 *The goring ox*

If an ox, as it went along the street, gored a man and so caused his death, there is no ground for claim in that case. If a man's ox is habitually given to goring, and the man's local authority has notified him that it is habitually given to goring, and he has not protected its horns (*86*) (nor) restrained (the movements of) his ox, and that ox has gored a man of the 'gentleman' class and caused his death, he shall pay half a mina of silver. If (the man killed) is a gentleman's slave, he shall pay one-third of a mina of silver.

It may have been noticed that so far the word 'code' has been avoided in connection with the legal contents of the Stele of Hammurabi. This has been deliberate, to avoid prejudicing the issue of what the legal work concerned actually was. The term 'code', defined in *The Concise Oxford Dictionary* as 'a body of laws so arranged as to avoid inconsistency and overlapping', implies the systematic treatment of law on the basis of a particular theory of law. Can this term properly be applied to the laws of Hammurabi? The most recent substantial discussion of this problem has been that of Professor F. R. Kraus of Leiden, and what follows is largely based on his published article.

It will be clear, from the examples of laws quoted, that every legal pronouncement in the laws of Hammurabi is given in the form 'If such-and-such has happened, then such-and-such will result.' Their very form suggests that they may be different in some way from laws drawn up in the 'Thou shalt not' form, which are obviously general prohibitions. What we have been referring to as 'the laws' of Hammurabi are not in the stele itself called by a word meaning 'laws', and indeed there is not even a word for the conception 'law' in the language of the period concerned. The 'laws' are in fact referred to by a term which means 'judgements' or 'legal decisions'. It was one of the most important duties of an ancient Semitic ruler to give a just decision in disputes, and the term used indicates that King Hammurabi's 'laws' were intended as decisions of this kind. This does not mean, however, that the central part of the text of the stele is a straightforward collection of royal verdicts. We have many examples of records of specific lawsuits, and their normal form is quite different from that of the sections of the 'laws' of Hammurabi. There are other reasons for regarding the legal core of the text of Hammurabi's Stele as more than a simple collection of decisions about cases which had actually been brought to the King's notice. There are some groups of laws in which some sections would seem to be decisions about real cases which had actually come before the King, whilst others seem to have been invented as elaborations or analogies. A group of 'laws' which shows this clearly is a passage dealing with the consequence of a man's striking a woman and causing a miscarriage. The first 'decision' concerns the straightforward case of a man striking a free woman, who in consequence suffered a miscarriage. Following this are elaborations in which the woman struck was a low-caste woman or a slave, and others in which the women of the three social classes had died in consequence of the blow. Unless it is assumed that the beating-up of pregnant women was a popular Babylonian pastime, Hammurabi can hardly have had to decide separately upon each of these six circumstances, which leads us to the conclusion that some at least of these particular decisions were upon hypothetical cases. To this degree there is some justification for applying the term 'code' to the contents of the Stele of Hammurabi.

Each section of the 'laws' was not simply a decision in one specific case, but was intended to serve as a basis for the treatment of every similar case that arose throughout the land, both during the reign of Hammurabi and thereafter. They were not so much laws as precedents, even though in some cases fictitious ones. As Professor Kraus puts it, the so-called 'laws' were 'specimen decisions, patterns for good administration of justice'. This is clear from the specific advice which Hammurabi offered to his successors:

> To the end of days, for ever, may the king who happens to be in the land observe the words of justice which I have inscribed on my stele; ... if that man has the sanction (of the gods) and so is able to give his land justice, let him pay heed to the words which I have written on my stele, and let that stele show him the accustomed way, the way to follow, the land's judgements which I have judged and the land's decisions which I have decided.

Did the contents of the Stele of Hammurabi represent a reform? This is a question which has been much discussed, and the answer depends upon what one understands by 'reform'. If one means, was Hammurabi attempting to make deliberate alterations in the social structure and general legal practice of his land, the answer is certainly that in this sense the 'laws' were not a reform. On the other hand, there had undoubtedly been differences of practice in some matters in different parts of Babylonia, and it is a reasonable supposition (though one which has not yet actually been proved) that Hammurabi wished to secure a uniform pattern of justice throughout his land. If this was so, then for some parts of the

87 Audience hall of King of Eshnunna

country at least, some of the decisions are likely to have represented changes radical enough to be regarded as reforms.

The 'laws' of Hammurabi did not arise in a vacuum. There was already a long tradition not only of kings giving decisions in specific cases but also of their having collections of their decisions committed to writing. Four principal collections of 'laws' earlier than Hammurabi are known, the most extensive and best preserved of these being what are known as the 'laws of Eshnunna'. Eshnunna was a kingdom, centred on a city of the same name, which flourished in the Diyala region during the two centuries before Hammurabi unified Babylonia (1761 B.C.). Amongst the towns of this kingdom was one called Shaduppum, now represented by a small mound called Tell Harmal on the outskirts of Baghdad. It was at this site that Iraqi archaeologists, excavating shortly after the Second World War, found two copies, inscribed on clay tablets, of the collection of laws referred to. Damage at vital points has destroyed the evidence which might have given an exact date for the original compilation of the collection of laws, but there are good grounds for the conclusion that these laws originated at least a century earlier than the time of Hammurabi.

In the laws of Eshnunna the arrangement shows significant differences from that of the Stele of Hammurabi. There is no elaborate prologue, its place being taken by a date. Following this comes a tariff of prices, in the following form:

147

1 *gur* of barley for 1 shekel of silver;
3 *qa* of refined oil for 1 shekel of silver;
....
6 minas of wool for 1 shekel of silver;
2 *gur* of salt for 1 shekel of silver.

Some commentators call this a tariff of *maximum* prices, but this makes certain unproven assumptions about the nature of the ancient economy. It seems more likely that these were fixed prices laid down in an attempt to give stability to the economy, rather than maximum prices controlled in an attempt to protect consumers.

A list of prices is also found in the laws of Hammurabi, but there it is by no means so prominent. Elsewhere there are other fragments of official price lists. Such details are significant pointers to the origin of the collections of royal 'laws'. They seem to suggest that originally there would be promulgated an official price list of staple commodities, and that gradually there would be appended to this records of other royal decisions on points arising from typical economic and social problems. The laws of Eshnunna show the result in a fairly rudimentary stage with the price tariff at the beginning; Hammurabi's laws are cast in a framework of considerable literary sophistication, and merely retain a few traces of the price tariff at the very end.

The way in which decisions upon particular cases could come to be added to the original price list is illustrated in the sections of the laws of Eshnunna directly following the price list of commodities. These sections concern rates of hire of wagons and ships, and the wages of the wagoner or boatman. The actual text reads:

§3 For a wagon with its oxen and its driver, the hire is 1 *pan* and 4 *seah* of barley; if in silver, its hire is one-third of a shekel. He shall drive it for the whole day.
§4 The hire of a boat is 2 *qa* (of barley) per *gur* (of hold space); 1 *qa* (of barley) is the hire of the boatman. He shall drive it for the whole day.
§5 If a boatman is negligent and sinks the boat, he shall pay in full for as much (cargo) as he sinks.

It seems a reasonable conclusion that §§3 and 4 were originally closely related to the list of commodity prices. §5 will then have represented a royal decision arising out of a boatman's claim under

148

§4, when the hirer of some boat had refused to pay at the prescribed rate, on the ground that the boat had come to grief and caused him loss.

Another instance of the same kind is provided by §§7–9. Here first of all the wages of agricultural labourers of different kinds are laid down. Then follows a decision upon a case related to this, where a labourer, hired under the terms laid down, had been paid in advance and then failed to turn up to do his work.

There is no space to give extensive quotations from particular sections of the laws of Eshnunna, and it is largely unnecessary, since about three-quarters of the laws of Eshnunna are very similar to laws in the Stele of Hammurabi. The details sometimes differ slightly, but with one major exception there are no basic differences of attitude. The exception occurs in the laws dealing with assault, for which at Eshnunna the penalty would at first sight appear to come nearer to modern practice than does either the 'code' of Hammurabi or the Old Testament legislation, both of which lay down the principle of 'an eye for an eye'. In the laws of Eshnunna the penalty takes the form of a fine, thus:

§42 If a man bites a man's nose and so severs it, he shall pay one mina of silver. For an eye, one mina; for a tooth, half a mina; for an ear, half a mina; for a blow on the face he shall pay ten shekels of silver. §43 If a man has severed a man's finger, he shall pay two-thirds of a mina of silver. . . . §45 If he has broken (a man's) foot, he shall pay half a mina of silver.

However, at the end of these sections there is a further section, unfortunately damaged on both extant tablets, which may reasonably be restored to read:

§48 And in addition, in cases with penalties from one-third of a mina to one mina, they shall try the man. If it is a capital matter, it is a matter for the King.

This is a clear indication that the payment of damages did not necessarily settle the affair. Whether a man tried in these circumstances and found guilty of assault was mutilated or put to death is not certain, but the possibility is not to be excluded. It would certainly be misleading to draw hasty conclusions about the allegedly more humane tone of these laws and certain other (Sumerian) laws which specify a financial penalty for assault. It may well have been taken for granted in all such cases that the damages paid by the man guilty of assault were additional to a traditionally accepted physical punishment.

One further law from Eshnunna, not paralleled in the 'code' of Hammurabi, is worth quoting, since it reflects a practice also known from one of the most famous stories in the Old Testament. The law in question reads (according to Professor A. Goetze's interpretation of several words of uncertain meaning):

§25 If a man offers service in the house of a (potential) father-in-law, and his (potential) father-in-law accepts him in bondage and then gives his daughter to another man, the father of the girl shall return twofold the bride-price which he received (in the form of service).

The parallel in the situation to that of Jacob serving Laban seven years for Rachel, only to be tricked at the end (*Genesis* xxix 15–30), cannot be missed, though it may be added that Laban claimed (*Genesis* xxix 26) that according to the customary law of the Haran region he was justified in acting as he did towards Jacob.

As already mentioned, in addition to the laws of Eshnunna there are known at least three other collection of laws of earlier date than the code of Hammurabi. Two of these, the laws respectively of the rulers Ur-Nammu (2113–2096 B.C.) and Lipit-Ishtar (1934–1924 B.C.) are in Sumerian. The third group referred to comprises a few sections of the laws of an Assyrian merchant colony which existed in Anatolia (eastern Turkey) about 1900 B.C.; these laws, written in the Assyrian dialect of Akkadian, concern commercial and administrative procedure.

From the Near East in the period between Hammurabi and Moses come some Hittite laws (which fall outside the scope of this work) and some further Assyrian laws, datable to between 1450 and 1250 B.C. The most extensive section preserved from these latter laws is mainly concerned with legislation involving women. The matters concerned may be summarised as follows: sacrilegious theft; blasphemy or sedition; illicit sale or loan by a woman of her husband's property, or theft from another man; assault by a woman; assault upon a woman; murder; rape of a married woman; adultery; accusation of immorality against a man's wife; slander against a man's wife or a man; homosexuality amongst men; assault by a man upon a woman, causing miscarriage; employment of married woman as business agent; procuring; harbouring a runaway wife; inheritance; espousal; various forms of marriage; divorce; married women to be veiled; prostitutes and slave-girls to be unveiled; procedure for marriage in specified circumstances; creditor's rights of corporal punishment over man or woman held as pledge for a debt; remarriage of woman whose husband is presumed dead; provision for a widow; treatment of men or women accused of black magic; limitation of creditor's rights over girl held as security for debt; [damaged]; assault by a man upon various classes of woman, causing miscarriage; a woman's self-induced abortion; rape of a virgin; fornication by a virgin; administrative procedure for inflicting corporal punishment or mutilation upon a married women.

In general, although these laws are several centuries later than those of Hammurabi, the penalties show a more barbarous spirit, in many cases involving mutilation. The following extracts give some idea of the contents and the tone of the Assyrian laws:

§3 If a man is ill or dead, and his wife has stolen something from his house and delivered it either to a (free) man or to a (free) woman or to anyone else, the man's wife and the receivers shall be put to death. And if a married woman, whose husband is in sound health, has stolen something from her husband's house and delivered it either to a (free) man or to a (free) woman or to anyone else, the man shall charge his wife and shall impose the punishment; and the receiver . . . shall give up the stolen thing, and a punishment like that which the man imposed on his wife shall be imposed on the receiver.

§15 If a man has caught a man with his wife and has then brought a charge against him and proved it against him, both of them shall be put to death; there is no guilt in this. If he has caught (him) and brought (him) before either the King or the judges, and has brought a charge against him and proved it against him, if the woman's husband kills his wife, he shall likewise kill the man; if he cuts off his wife's nose, he shall make the man a eunuch and shall slash the whole of his face; but if he lets his wife off, the man shall be let off.

§27 If a woman is living in her father's house and her husband regularly goes in (to her there), any settlement which her husband has delivered to her is his (property), he may take it. He may not lay claim to anything belonging to her father's house. [This probably refers to an ancient type of marriage in which the woman continued to live in the household in which she had grown up, being visited by her husband only at night. There are still parts of the world in which this kind of marriage is usual.]

§34 If a man has taken a widow, but has not drawn up a contract for her, if she lives in his house for two years, she (becomes) a wife; she shall not (be compelled to) go away.

§40 Wives, whether married women or widows. . . , who go out into the street, shall not have their heads uncovered. . . . A member of the harem who goes out with her mistress into the street shall be veiled. A sacred prostitute whom a husband has married shall have her head covered in the street, but one whom a husband has not married shall have her head uncovered in the street; she shall not veil herself. A common harlot shall not veil herself; her head shall be uncovered. Anyone who sees a common harlot veiled shall arrest(?) her. He shall produce men as witnesses and bring her to the Palace. They may not take her jewellery but the man who arrested her may take her clothing. They shall beat her fifty strokes with rods, and they shall pour pitch on her head. And if a man has seen a common harlot veiled and has let her go and has not brought her to the Palace, they shall beat that man fifty strokes with rods; the man who denounced him shall take his clothing; they shall pierce his ears and thread (them) with a cord and shall tie it behind him; he shall do service for the King for one complete month. . . . [The law goes on to say that slave-girls must likewise not be veiled; the penalty for a slave-girl's contravention of this regulation was to have her ears cut off. A man who failed in his duty of reporting an offending slave-girl was liable to the penalty prescribed above.]

§59 Leaving aside the penalties relating to a married woman which are inscribed on the tablet, a man may flog his wife, pull out her hair, split and injure her ears. There is no legal guilt (involved) in it.

In addition to those Middle Assyrian laws dealt with above, there are less extensive remains of other groups of laws of the same period, the two principal tablets dealing respectively with land tenure and commercial transactions.

It is almost unnecessary to point out that the average citizen of ancient Mesopotamia, like his modern counterpart, was usually concerned not with the theoretical aspects of law and its origin but with the manner in which it operated to protect his own interests. If, for example, a person found that his neighbour was claiming rights over a field which he considered his own property, what steps could he take to have his rights protected? We know something about the answer to this question, as there are many documents dealing with problems of this kind. Let us consider a particular case from the reign of Hammurabi's successor, Samsu-iluna.

A man Ibbi-Shamash fell out with a priestess Naram-tani over the ownership of a plot of land. Naram-tani had inherited the plot from an aunt Nishi-inishu, also a priestess, who, Naram-tani had always understood, had bought it from the father of Ibbi-Shamash fifty-two years before. Ibbi-Shamash now claimed, however, that the plot his father had actually sold to Nishi-inishu had been a smaller one, and that Nishi-inishu had wrongfully taken possession of the larger plot in question. Ibbi-Shamash and Naram-tani were unable to agree upon the matter and so they took the case to the Registrar and judges of their city, Sippar. The officials duly heard the claims of both parties and would certainly have heard the testimony of the original witnesses to the sale had they been available, but there is no mention of such witnesses, not surprisingly in view of the half century which had elapsed. The judges therefore simply settled the matter by examining the original tablet of sale drawn up over fifty years before. This might at first telling appear to give ample scope for forgery by the family which had had the keeping of the original tablet, but the ingenious procedure with contract tablets at this period prevented this. The procedure was to write out a clay tablet with the terms of contract, the contracting parties and witnesses then rolling their seals over the blank portions of the tablet. The scribe drawing up the document would then take another piece of clay, flatten it out, and fold it over the original tablet to make a sealed envelope of the same shape as the original tablet. On this envelope would then be written the terms of the original contract, cylinder seals being rolled over the document as before (*88*). The text on the envelope would of course be subject to

88 A cylinder-seal impression

deliberate falsification or obliteration by wear, but the original inner tablet could not be touched without breaking the envelope. What the judges did in the case in question was to break the envelope and read the intact tablet within. They found that the plot of land bought by Nishi-inishu fifty-two years before was clearly stated to be the size of the plot currently claimed by her niece Naram-tani, who therefore won the case. A document was drawn up giving details of the case and the decision and concluding with a clause forbidding Ibbi-Shamash to reopen the case against Naram-tani. It is from the actual document drawn up at the end of the case that we are acquainted with all the foregoing details.

Naturally there were many cases in which citizens fell out with each other in which the truth could not be ascertained in this simple way by reference to written documents. In such cases the parties concerned came before the judges, each party telling his story and bringing witnesses who were prepared to swear to the truth of it. At some periods free citizens in general could sit with the judges to constitute a body known as the Assembly, which may have served as a kind of primitive jury. There was no prosecuting or defending counsel, and there was no cross-examination of witnesses, the telling of the truth being ensured as far as possible by making witnesses and litigants take the oath by the gods. If there was an irreconcilable conflict between the evidence of the two parties, the judges then had recourse to the ordeal, whereby the accused person was required to be judged by the River-god. This meant that he was required to jump into the river, which if he were guilty of a false oath would drown him. This might appear to put all the risk on the accused person, but in fact if the accused person went through with the ordeal procedure (which he would presumably only dare to do if he were convinced of his own innocence) and came safely back, his accuser would be put to death. Amongst the Mari letters there is one which makes this quite clear. One King wrote to another saying that he was sending two men under escort, accused of some crime, and asking that they should be submitted to the river ordeal. The King making the request explained that he had detained the accuser, and that if the two men accused came safely back, he would have the accuser burnt to death. If on the other hand the accused men drowned, their estates would be handed over to the man who had accused them.

The manner in which fear of the consequences of a false oath might produce the truth is shown by the following document, which comes from the city of Nuzi, in eastern Assyria, about 1400 B.C.:

> Tekhip-tilla son of Pukhisheni came before the judges in a lawsuit with Tilliya son of Taya.
> Tilliya the oxherd had flayed three oxen of Tekhip-tilla in the town of Katiri. Tekhip-tilla's witnesses spoke to this effect before the judges: 'Tilliya flayed three oxen of Tekhip-tilla without (the authority of) the cattle-overseer(?), and he was caught over the three oxen, whilst he was flaying them.'
> So the judges said to Tilliya: 'Go! Take the oath of the gods against the witnesses and the cattle-overseer(?).' But he was unwilling to take the oath of the gods. Tilliya turned back from (submitting the case to) the gods. So Tekhip-tilla was successful in the lawsuit and they imposed on Tilliya (the payment of) three oxen to Tekhip-tilla.
> Seal of A, seal of B, seal of C, seal of D, seal of E; hand of X son of Y [this final entry indicates the scribe].

As to penalties for criminal conduct, the death penalty is frequently referred to in the laws of Hammurabi, whilst the Assyrian laws mention, as will have been noticed, several forms of mutilation as penalties. One text sums up the matter of legal penalties by saying that a man who commits a felony is either executed, or flayed, or blinded, or fettered, or thrown into prison. Often, however, the system was not as brutal in practice as this might suggest. A money payment might be acceptable in place of punishment, and we find mention of such settlements as 'silver received in lieu of the cutting off of [so-and-so's] hand, and in lieu of the imprisonment of [so-and-so]'. In general, prolonged close imprisonment was not usual; this was not, probably, on any humanitarian grounds but mainly because if a person had the right to restrict another's liberty it would be more efficient to make him a slave and put him to work.

Chapter VIII

NEBUCHADNEZZAR'S BABYLON

THE time of Babylon's greatest material wealth and splendour, and the period which is reflected in much of the later tradition about Babylon, was the reign of Nebuchadnezzar (605–562 B.C.). We are fortunate in having a fair amount of information about the city at this period, not only from Biblical and Greek tradition, but also from Nebuchadnezzar's own building inscriptions, and from the business, legal and administrative records of his reign. Important information has also been obtained from the excavation of the city itself (*91*), notably in the dig directed by the German, Robert Koldewey, between 1899 and 1917. Taken together, these strands of evidence give us a fairly clear outline of life in the Babylonian capital under Nebuchadnezzar II, though of course there are many details which we do not yet know and some which we may never know.

At the time of Nebuchadnezzar the city of Babylon spread out on both sides of the Euphrates. What we may call the 'old city' was the part on the east bank, and this was somewhat larger than the 'new city' opposite. Close by the east bank and in the centre of the city as a whole stood Etemenanki, 'House of the platform of Heaven and Earth', the great seven-storeyed ziggurat or temple-tower (*90*), already very old but splendidly rebuilt at this time. This was possibly the original behind the 'tower of Babel' story of the Bible (*Genesis* xi 1–9), though of course the Biblical tradition relates to a period over 2000 years before Nebuchadnezzar. This great tower, with a small temple on its summit, rose to a height of almost 300 feet and dominated the view across the plain for many miles around. The dimensions varied at different re-buildings, but excavations show its base at its maximum extent to have formed a square with sides of about 300 feet. This ziggurat's main mass was of trodden clay, though there was a casing of burnt brick nearly 50 feet thick. A staircase about 30 feet wide led up to the first and second stages; how the higher stages were reached is not certain, but presumably there were further staircases or ramps.

Etemenanki stood in an enclosure surrounded by a continuous line of brick-built chambers or double walls. Some of these chambers were certainly store-rooms. Others were probably houses for priests and other persons engaged in the service of religion, or perhaps (some people have suggested) lodgings for pilgrims.

Just to the south of the Etemenanki enclosure, and intimately associated with it, was the great temple-complex of Esagila, 'House of the Raised Head'. This contained not only the principal shrine sacred to the city-god Marduk (otherwise called Bel, 'The Lord'), but also others sacred to Marduk's son Nabu and a number of other deities. We have accounts of Esagila and Etemenanki both from Greek writers and from cuneiform tablets, one of the latter giving a detailed account of the measurements of both structures.

Inside Esagila the main chapel of Marduk was a chamber measuring some 66 feet by 132. This must have presented a scene of dazzling splendour, for, to quote simply one detail, Nebuchadnezzar himself records that he overlaid the whole of its interior, including the rafters, with gold. On a pedestal inside the chapel stood golden images of Marduk and his consort Sarpanitum, whilst images of divine attendants stood on either side of the supreme pair. These attendants included hairdressers for Sarpanitum, a butler and a baker, a door-keeper, and dogs. Statues of winged creatures called Kurub (whence our word 'Cherub') guarded the entrance. All these images were heavily decorated with gold and precious stones and dressed in rich raiment, but except for glimpses from the courtyard the ordinary Babylonian had to take this on hearsay, for it is unlikely that at the period of Nebuchadnezzar anyone other than the King, the Crown Prince and certain priests ever entered the inner shrine.

There were other temples in the city quite distinct from Esagila. Within the temples the usual (though not the invariable) layout was as follows. The god's statue stood in the middle of one long wall of an oblong chapel, and in the wall opposite was a doorway into an ante-chamber. The ante-chamber was very similar in shape to the main chapel and ran parallel to it. In the wall of the ante-chamber farthest from the chapel was another doorway giving access from the main courtyard, so that when both the ante-chamber door and the chapel door were open the populace could see through to the statue of the god himself. In the case of Marduk's shrine the doors opened towards a point a little to the north of east, as befitted a sun-god, though some other temples had quite different orientations. At the sides and back of the ante-chamber and chapel and around the courtyard there was a series of other chambers, used no doubt as store-rooms for the equipment used in the cult.

The temple-complexes themselves did not mark the whole of the piety of the Babylonians, for along many of the streets, particularly at the approaches to the temples, at the city gates and at cross-roads, were to be found small altars. These amounted, according to the cuneiform texts listing such things, to nearly 400, of which some have been found in excavations. In addition to these there were, according to the same series of texts, nearly a thousand roadside shrines scattered about the city.

In the northern part of the old city, just inside the inner walls, stood the principal palace of Nebuchadnezzar. As was usual in the ancient Near East, this was not only a royal residence but also a garrison and an administrative centre. Basically this palace (which went back to a period long before Nebuchadnezzar) was built round a series of five courtyards, used respectively (going from east to west) for the garrison, the secretariat, the State rooms, the King's private quarters, and the women's apartments or harem. In the women's apartments there lived not only Nebuchadnezzar's queen but also concubines sent to the King from all parts of the Empire. This was of course usual with ancient Oriental monarchs. One might imagine that with so many women, shut away with no company but their own, and with most of them sexually frustrated, strife and quarrelling sometimes broke out in the royal harem—and it did. We know this without any doubt as we have a cuneiform text (earlier than the time of Nebuchadnezzar) laying down regulations to deal with such problems in a royal harem.

It is hardly possible to discuss the Babylon of Nebuchadnezzar without mentioning the famous Hanging Gardens which he is credited with planting there(92). The difficulty is to disentangle fact from legend. Unfortunately, although there are plenty of references to the Hanging Gardens in classical authors, indicating that there must have been some striking piece of landscape gardening in the city, there is little if any evidence of them from cuneiform texts of the period. However, the classical writers must have had some basis for their reports and the Hanging Gardens cannot be dismissed out of hand as figments of the imagination. According to the classical writers, the gardens were installed by a king to please a Persian concubine who was depressed by the unbroken

89 The Ishtar Gate at Babylon
A reconstruction by Robert Koldewey

90 The enclosure of Etemenanki and Esagila in Babylon
A reconstruction by E. Unger

91 The Processional Way, Babylon, near the Ishtar Gate

92 The Hanging Gardens of Babylon (Koldewey's reconstruction)

flatness and longed for her native mountains. It was supposed to have been built near the river on a foundation of arched vaults, and to have risen in a series of terraces to a height of 75 feet. The whole structure was then waterproofed with bitumen, baked brick, and lead, with the object of keeping the vaults underneath it dry. Finally the terraces were covered with earth to a depth sufficient to support even large trees. Trees were then planted and provided with a constant supply of water from the Euphrates by irrigation machines.

There is some archaeological evidence which could be related to the classical traditions. In the north-eastern corner of the palace mentioned above, the archaeologists found a structure which seemed to have no parallel elsewhere. Basically this structure consisted of two rows of seven vaulted chambers beneath ground level. The central chambers had thicker walls than the outer ones, and this might mean that the central chambers had been intended to bear a greater weight than the outer ones. This is just what the situation would have been if the vaulted chambers had been the sub-structure bearing the weight of a terraced hill of earth, arranged as described by the classical authors.

Whether or not it was the Hanging Gardens which were supported by these vaulted chambers, the chambers themselves were certainly used as offices or store-rooms, since tablets have been found in them dealing with grain issues. Amongst these tablets were some actually referring to the Jehoiachin King of Judah taken prisoner by Nebuchadnezzar to Babylon (*2 Kings* xxiv 15). Because of this, some people have suggested that the underground chambers were really dungeons for political prisoners, but this does not follow. One would expect to find lists of rations issued to prisoners either in the records office or in the stores, not in the prisoners' cells.

Like every city, Babylon was recognised by its inhabitants as being made up of a number of distinct districts, the names and characteristics of some of which we know. Roughly speaking, the temples, palaces and other public buildings were in the western half of the old city, with the residential quarters in the eastern half and across the Euphrates in the new city (though the new city also contained several temples)(*94*). Its main streets were laid out in a direction from north-west to south-east, the object of this being to give the city the full benefit of the prevailing north-west wind to carry away smells and keep the temperature down. The streets of Babylon, of which twenty-four are mentioned in one text, bore names like 'Marduk shepherd of his land', 'He hears from afar', and 'May the enemy not have victory'. The last was the name of a section of a road which entered the city through the Ishtar Gate in the north wall, just east of the palace (*1*). This road is now usually

93 A dragon from the Ishtar Gate

known as the Processional Way, from the fact of its being the principal street used by Marduk when the priests took him through the city on ceremonial occasions. It was an efficient piece of road engineering; up to 66 feet wide in parts, it consisted of a brick foundation covered with asphalt to form a bed for large paving slabs of limestone. The north approach to the Ishtar Gate took the traveller between high walls decorated with rows of lions, sixty on each side, in red, white and yellow enamelled tiles (*89*). A similar technique was employed inside the Ishtar Gate itself, where bulls and dragons were depicted (*93*). From the Ishtar Gate the Processional Way ran parallel to the Euphrates half-way through the old city and then turned west to pass between Etemenanki and Esagila towards the river, where it passed over a bridge into the western half of Babylon. The remains of this bridge have been found, and it proves to have been built on piles made of bricks bonded with bitumen. These piles were 30 feet wide and 30 feet apart, except near the western bank where the gap was 60 feet, to facilitate the passage of ships. The piles were roughly boat-shaped, their sides curving inwards to a point at the upstream end to cut down resistance to the current. The classical writers speak of this as a stone bridge, which presumably indicates that the piles were crowned with stone blocks which carried the bridge itself, running from one pile to the next on heavy wooden beams. The course of the Processional Way in the western half of Babylon can only be guessed, since the Euphrates has changed its bed and now flows through the middle of that part.

Winding through the old city, making a wide curve from its inlet from the Euphrates in the north-west corner to the point at which it passed through the inner wall in the south-east, was the ancient canal Libil-hegalla, whose name meant 'May it bring prosperity'. The origin of this canal may well have gone back to Hammurabi 1200 years before, but it was Nebuchadnezzar who restored it, lining its bed with bitumen and burnt brick. Other less venerable canals brought prosperity to the gardens and orchards of the new city on the west bank and to the suburbs on both sides.

The whole city was protected by formidable fortifications. Around the main built-up area on both sides of the Euphrates ran a powerful defensive system consisting of a double wall of unbaked brick with an encircling moat. The inner part of this double wall was 21 feet thick, with towers regularly placed every 59 feet. Separated by a space of 24 feet was the outer part of the wall,

12 feet thick, with towers every 67 feet. Outside the walls came the moat, with its bed lined with burnt brick and bitumen; the source of its water was of course the Euphrates. Entrance to the city was through the Ishtar Gate or one of seven other powerfully fortified great gates, which all had massive doors armoured in bronze. The bridges over the moat which must have existed in normal times would no doubt be dismantled in times of emergency.

As a further protection to the city, Nebuchadnezzar constructed a great outer fortification, consisting of another double wall which, starting from the east bank of the Euphrates a mile-and-a-half north of the Ishtar Gate, ran in a south-easterly direction to a point level with Esagila, and then turned south-westwards to meet the Euphrates again, a quarter of a mile south of the inner defensive system. This outer double wall was limited to the protection of the old city.

The total population of Babylon at the time of Nebuchadnezzar is not certainly known, but there are various pointers to assist in making an intelligent guess. The area of the city within the inner walls was about one and two-thirds square miles or slightly more than 1000 acres. On the basis of populations of more recent Oriental cities, which have generally been found to be between 150 and 200 to the acre, this would indicate a population of up to 200,000. Such a figure would be of the right order to fit in reasonably well with the Biblical passage (*Jonah* iv 11) which estimates the population of Nineveh, a comparable capital, at 120,000. Another pointer is the statement of one of the classical writers that Babylon could lodge 200,000 men for defence, an estimate presumably based on the known population in normal times. Such populations meant that there was no urban sprawl, and densely inhabited though parts of particular cities may have been, all were set in the midst of open country. City dwellers were still not divorced from the countryside and from acquaintance with animals of the wild, and we have (though not specifically from Babylon) reference to a gazelle, notoriously a timid creature, coming right up to the city gate. Elsewhere there is mention of a wild bull joining the domestic herd.

The population of Babylon was a very mixed one, both racially and socially. As to race, Nebuchadnezzar impressed labour gangs for his public works in Babylon from the whole of his Empire. Many of these were no doubt only too glad to return to their native lands when their task was over, but others certainly stayed for good in Babylon, either settling down with wives who had followed them from their homeland or marrying local women. Such foreign settlers were no more than the most recent importation of foreign blood. There were many other peoples who during the preceding centuries had been in the city, whether as conquerors, captives or just visitors, long enough to interbreed with Babylonian ladies. Amongst these were Hurrians, Cassites, Hittites, Elamites, an occasional Egyptian, Aramaeans, Assyrians, Chaldaeans, and, in the reign of Nebuchadnezzar himself, Jews. Babylon was a thoroughly mongrel city.

Socially there were two great divisions in the city, which to some extent cut across each other. One division was between free men and slaves, the other between temple personnel and laity. The temple personnel, who included people ranging from the lowest

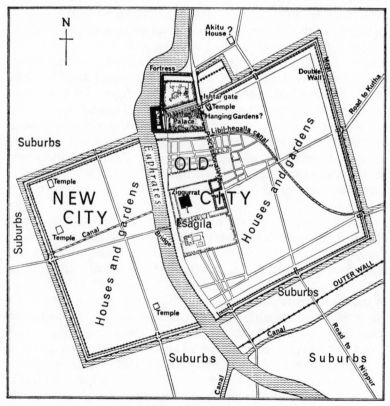

94 Plan of Babylon, sixth century B.C.

grade of slaves to high-ranking priests who could challenge the actions of the King himself, formed almost a State within a State. The temple of Esagila owned, and its officials administered, huge estates. Taken as a whole, the temples of Babylonia at this time probably owned at least half the total land of the country, and played a major part in the control of the national economy. The agents of the temple were responsible for a good deal of the external trade of Babylonia. From Babylon such men might travel to Syria to buy olive oil or timber, or to Asia Minor for alum and gall-nuts for dyeing, or for metal ores. Payment by the temples would be in the form of wool or barley. The goods bought from Syria or Asia Minor would be carried on pack-asses as far as the Euphrates, and then shipped direct to Babylon. Trade was also conducted between Esagila and the temples of other Babylonian cities, mainly by river, the ships used being in some cases owned by the temples and in others hired from private owners: their maximum capacity at this time seems to have been about sixty tons.

Some of the farms belonging to Esagila were let out to farmers who paid rent in the form of a share of the produce, whilst others were worked by the temple's own slaves. It was on the farms that the majority of the temple slaves were employed, as agricultural labourers engaged in the seasonal round of ploughing, sowing, reaping and threshing, as herdsmen to tend the temple flocks and herds, as fowlers and fishermen, or as blacksmiths and carpenters to repair the ploughs and other equipment. Above all, there were gangs, both of temple slaves and hired labourers, who worked in the unceasing effort to keep the canals in good repair for irrigation and shipping.

Amongst personnel not belonging to the temple, the lowest category from the legal point of view was of course the slave, though the standard of living of a slave in a wealthy household might be a good deal higher than that of a poor free man. Whether the lot of a particular private slave was better or worse than that of his counterpart in temple ownership obviously depended upon the personal relationship between slave and master. Some masters were undoubtedly very hard men, who made their unfortunate slaves so desperate that they ran away. On the other hand, with an easy-going master, an ungrateful slave might become lazy, indolent and unmanageable, and we hear of one aging couple who had to take measures to bring a slave, presumably of this kind, under the control of the temple-slave administration.

The duties of male private slaves mainly involved manual labour, and would depend to some extent upon the trade or craft of the owner. A female slave, when young, would probably act not only as a maid to

95 Products of the coppersmith: bronze safety-pins

the lady of the house but also as a concubine of either the master of the house or one of the teenage sons. Any children born to the slave-girl would become slaves unless the head of the family formally accepted them as his own children, which would probably only happen if his wife were childless. When the slave-girl grew old and ugly, she would come in for such duties as grinding the corn, drawing the water, and so on. The average household at the time of Nebuchadnezzar had two or three slaves, though of course an average does not tell the whole story: wealthy families might own considerably more and poor families none. We do find some wealthy families owning a hundred or more slaves, but most of these would have been used on the land or in workshops and would not have been included in the household.

Free men might engage in a wide range of crafts or professions, though this is not the same as saying that any particular man had a wide choice of craft or profession. The hereditary principle was very strong, and the chances were very much that a man would follow in his father's footsteps. Amongst the crafts and professions we find mentioned in the Babylon of Nebuchadnezzar are mat-makers, weavers, stone-masons, laundrymen, goldsmiths, fishermen, boatmen, leather-workers and shoemakers, confectioners, bakers, brewers, oil-pressers, brickmakers, blacksmiths and coppersmiths, millers, fowlers, carpenters, canal-diggers, and sheep-shearers, to mention but a few.

Training for such crafts and professions was mainly by apprenticeship, either to a private master-craftsman or with a guild. Formal education was probably available in association with the temples for those wishing to enter the learned professions based on scribal craft, but we know little or nothing of the details of this at this period.

At the apex of society was the royal court and the King, Nebuchadnezzar himself. Nebuchadnezzar is most famous as a brilliant strategist and general, but nothing will be said here about his army or his military activities, as the details would be too similar to those of the Assyrian army discussed in Chapter V. Besides being a great soldier, Nebuchadnezzar was a great builder, and most of the palaces, temples, fortifications and canals of Babylon were restored during his reign.

Nebuchadnezzar's courtiers mainly comprised provincial governors, army commanders, diplomatists, foreign princes held as hostages, and members of the King's family and of other branches of the blood royal. Officials specifically mentioned as being at Nebuchadnezzar's Court included (to give literal translations of their titles) the Chief Baker, the Chief of the Military Contingents (*i.e.* the Commander-in-Chief), the Man over the Palace (*i.e.* the Lord Chamberlain), the Secretary of the Crown Prince, and the Representative for the Harem. Unless human nature has radically changed, this last-mentioned official must have been a eunuch; possibly some of the other officials were too.

The general layout of Nebuchadnezzar's principal palace has already been mentioned, and the way of life in it was probably not markedly different from that at Mari 1200 years before. We may therefore leave the palace and turn to see how the ordinary Babylonian free man lived at this time. We may consider first the kind of house he lived in.

One must not expect a private house in ancient Babylon to be basically similar to a house in a modern English or American suburb. In building a house, the Babylonian had two objects in view. He wanted privacy, particularly in respect to his womenfolk, and he wanted a refuge from the burning Babylonian sun. The privacy he obtained by having the outer walls of the house almost blank and by arranging for the rooms to open only on to a central courtyard. The protection against the sun he obtained

96 House of the Nebuchadnezzar period

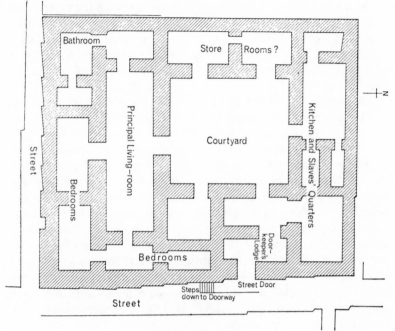

Bathroom

Store   Rooms ?

Principal Living-room

Courtyard

Kitchen and Slaves' Quarters

Bedrooms

Street

Bedrooms

Door-keeper's Lodge

Steps down to Doorway   Street Door

Street

97 Plan of a house

by making the walls of his house of mud brick, up to 6 feet thick. This may seem to be excessively massive, but those who have lived in Baghdad in houses built to flimsy European standards instead of traditional Mesopotamian ones know how ineffective walls of normal thickness are against the sun there, if electrical air-conditioning happens to break down.

In thinking of a Babylonian private house we have to imagine a central courtyard with groups of rooms leading off on every side (*97*). The largest room was always the one immediately to the south of the courtyard. There was nothing symbolic about this: the point was simply that the principal living-room had to have its entrance (which of course had to be from the courtyard and not from the street) facing north, away from the sun. The size of such a room ranged from about 18 feet by 8 in the smallest houses to 45 feet by 17 in the largest. Usually this large room also had doorways in its three other walls. These led to a series of subsidiary rooms along the back and sides of the main room, in three non-connected suites. Smaller houses might, of course, be without some of these subsidiary rooms, whilst bigger houses, on the other hand, might have more than one courtyard, each with corresponding groups of rooms around it. Big houses of this kind were obviously the property of wealthy people, and the additional courtyards, with the rooms around them, probably served as houses for married sons.

The surface of courtyards and the floors of rooms would usually be of burnt brick, sometimes finished off with a layer of a composition of bitumen and powdered limestone. This must have been very similar to some of the flooring finishes used in post-war houses, though more durable, as some of it is still sound after 2500 years. It is likely that in the wealthier houses the floors were covered with woollen rugs, though in poorer houses some of the floors were simply of trodden earth covered with no moré than reed mats. The ceilings, probably whitewashed, as the walls certainly were, were of rafters of palm-wood, overlaid with reed matting, on the top of which, for insulation against the sun, there was a thick layer of mud. High in the walls of rooms, on the courtyard side where possible, but sometimes necessarily facing on to the street, were small ventilation openings, covered with terracotta grids(98) to keep out vermin as far as that was possible. This device was not always successful, and a Babylonian might wake up in the night to find that a snake had fallen on to his bed, having crept in through the ventilator shaft and crawled along the rafters.

According to the Greek traveller Herodotus, writing about a century after Nebuchadnezzar, many of the houses in Babylon were of three or four storeys. If this, or anything approaching it, was true of the time of Nebuchadnezzar, then the upper storeys may possibly have consisted of light timber structures, perhaps to ensure privacy to members of the household sleeping on the roof in the summer. There is no archaeological evidence of stairs to upper storeys, but this does not prove there were no upper storeys, as stairs

98 A terracotta grid to serve as a window

could well have been made of wood, which is far less likely to leave traces than stone or brick.

Whatever the form of the upper storeys, if any, the roofings of the house would certainly be mainly of horizontal timbers covered with a thick layer of mud. Flat mud roofs of this kind needed some sort of protection against rain, since although rainfall at Babylon amounts to only five inches a year, it all comes in one short season and frequently in two or three periods of very heavy rain. Thus it was necessary to get the water away from the flat roofs and the footings of the mud brick walls before it could do serious damage. For this purpose there were pottery drains, fixed vertically in the walls. These carried the water off from the roof down to street level, where it ran into a soakaway or sump consisting of a kind of pit lined with terracotta rings. This was also the normal means at Babylon of disposal of waste water from kitchen, bathroom and lavatory, though elsewhere in Mesopotamia, a good deal earlier, there had been some main drainage systems.

The outer walls of a private house were usually, except for an occasional ventilation grid and the outer door, unbroken and, as far as the general plan was concerned, quite straight. However, the monotony was often relieved by the walls being given what can best be described as a 'saw-toothed' form. That is to say, the outline would often be like this:

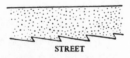

STREET

The brilliant sunlight of Babylon would thus produce on the blank buff-coloured or whitewashed walls alternate contrasting bands of light and shade. The street door (there would only be one) was framed in a vaulted archway in the wall, somewhere in the northern part of the house. Just inside the house from the street door there was a very small room for the door-keeper, who would of course be a slave, though a reliable and trusted one, as the security of the house depended on his vigilance. The person entering a private house had to be admitted by the door-keeper and then pass through at least two rooms before he reached the courtyard, which was of course the only means of approach to the main living-room in the south of the building. The Babylonians obviously liked domestic privacy, and the doors of the rooms leading from the

171

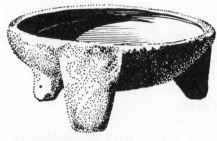

99 Basalt bowl for rubbing out grain

street doorway were always so arranged that even with the outer door open it was impossible to peep into the courtyard from the street. Even more than for the Englishman, the Babylonian's home was his castle.

The particular purpose of many of the rooms in a Babylonian house is a matter for intelligent guessing, though with some of them the presence of particular equipment or architectural features settles the matter. One group of rooms to the north of the courtyard usually contained the kitchen, pantries, and probably the slaves' quarters. The kitchen, one of the larger rooms, would have in one corner the cooking hearth, consisting of two brick platforms six inches or so apart at the bottom and sloping together to a narrow slit at the top, where pots and pans could be placed (*100*). For people who could afford it, the fuel used in such a hearth was mainly charcoal, generally from palm-wood, as no other wood was easily available for common use.

In the neighbourhood of the kitchen there were a number of large pottery jars for the storage of water, which was brought up from the river by the household slaves. These particular jars were unglazed, since it was a great advantage to have them slightly porous, so that the slight consequent evaporation would keep the water refreshingly cool. Similar jars, often lined with a coating of bitumen, were used for other kitchen stores such as barley, wheat and oil. The Babylonians liked stale beer and wine as little as we do, and these were kept in sealed jars. Kitchen utensils included such things as basins, bowls, sieves and cups, all made of terracotta, sometimes left in their yellowish-buff colour, sometimes glazed in blue, white or

100 A kitchen hearth

yellow (*101*). There were

101 Kitchen utensils

also terracotta chests for the rat-proof storage of various foods. Equipment would usually include mortars of baked clay or stone, used for pounding spices, a stone handmill for grinding the wheat or barley, and of course knives.

At the south end of the house one of the rooms behind the principal chamber was a bathroom. In this the floor, so built as to slope towards the centre, consisted of baked bricks overlaid with the usual composition of bitumen and powdered limestone, whilst the lower parts of the walls were also lined with baked brick. Beneath the lowest part of the floor in the centre of the room was a soakaway or sump of the type already described, into which the waste water from the bathroom flowed. According to the archaeologists who excavated Babylon, no traces of bath-tubs are found from the period of Nebuchadnezzar. This seems odd, since they were certainly used in other parts of Mesopotamia earlier, but possibly the typical Babylonian was content simply to take a shower by having a slave pour water over him, whilst he washed himself down with a kind of soap made of the ashes of certain plants mixed with fats.

The other rooms behind the main chamber and to its sides were probably the family bedrooms. The beds in them would be of wood, without headboards or footboards, very much like a divan

173

102 A pipe lamp

on short legs, with the horizontal part apparently of reed matting. The beds were usually put with the head against a wall, with a free space on both sides. Inside the bedrooms there were probably also chests in which clothes could be stored. These chests were often made of terracotta, though wealthier people might have had them made of wood.

In the main room it seems likely that there were, at least in the wealthier houses, rugs on the floor. There would be a table, and probably five or six wooden chairs with rush seats, since it was not the Babylonian idea of comfort to squat on the floor for meals or everyday tasks (*103–4*). Poorer people might sit on low pottery stools. Artificial light, when necessary, was provided at this time by small lamps with a wick, using olive oil as the fuel (*102*).

Babylonians who could afford it had four meals a day, a substantial breakfast, a light lunch, and a heavy meal and a light snack again in the evening. A meal began with a slave pouring water over the hands of those dining, into a basin beneath. The family group then sat round the table, and the head of the family said a grace calling upon certain gods. The food was then placed on the table, mainly in one large vessel, from which everyone helped himself, generally using fingers, though knives, forks and spoons were not unknown in ancient Babylonia. Largely the meal consisted of vegetable products. Beef, mutton and goat-meat were regular items

103 Assyrian table

104 Chair with a rush seat

of the diet of the gods, and also (contrary to the statement of some other books) of those Babylonians who could afford it, though the poorer people may seldom have eaten red meat, except at religious festivals. Pig-meat was taboo to all the gods, but humans still ate it, and since pigs wandered about the streets semi-wild as scavengers, poor people probably had the chance of eating pork much more often than they did beef. The Euphrates abounded (and still does) with fish of various edible species, some of them reaching a weight of 200 pounds, and we know there were professional fishermen at this time, so that we may conclude that fish was a common item of diet and, of course, a valuable source of protein (*105*). Of poultry and game, ducks, geese, pigeons and partridges had always been available, and the hen had been introduced a century or so before Nebuchadnezzar, so that it was probably quite common by this time. The fish may have been split open and grilled over a charcoal fire, whilst the meat and poultry were generally boiled in a pot to make a stew.

105 Fishing

The meat, fish and poultry have been mentioned first, but they formed, of course, except in the diet of the rich, only the luxury items. The main part of most meals, and the whole of many meals for poor people, consisted of vegetable products. The main source of carbohydrate was barley bread, made by slapping lumps of unleavened dough on to the inside of a large pot heated in a fire to form a primitive oven. A method which is basically the same as the Babylonian one is still used in Iraq, and it produces a slab of bread, very appetising when fresh, which looks rather like a pancake cooked crisp. Coarse barley meal was also cooked with water to produce a kind of porridge or gruel. Various puddings and cakes were made with a basis of such ingredients as flour, olive oil or sesame oil, date-syrup, and lard. Date-syrup was date juice

175

pressed out and allowed to evaporate to a semi-solid consistency; this, and dates in other forms, adequately took the place of the prepared sugar in our diet. Honey from bees was known, and the honey-bee had in fact been domesticated in Mesopotamia for several centuries by the time of Nebuchadnezzar, but the honey from bees was still of less economic importance than their wax. Amongst fruit and vegetables eaten may be mentioned onions, garlic, gherkins of various kinds, peas and beans, lettuces, radishes, pomegranates, figs, grapes, and apricots.

The main drink was beer, though cold water was by no means despised. Beer was available in many different varieties, depending upon the method of preparation and the particular herbs used to flavour it. Alcoholic beverages were also made from dates. Wine made from grapes had long been known, but it was more expensive than date-wine, as the better qualities of it had to be imported from cooler climates. A letter of this period contains a complaint about a consignment of wine which had been sent in a ship normally used for carrying bitumen; the stench of the bitumen had apparently tainted the wine.

After a meal the diners wiped their mouths on table-napkins, and the slaves again poured water over their hands. If it was the midday meal, the diners would then go to their bedrooms for a siesta, which was very necessary, since for much of the year the heat is intolerable in Iraq during the early afternoon: this was so commonly accepted that one of the Babylonian words for midday meant in fact 'the time of lying down'.

Herodotus gives us a detailed description of the clothing of a Babylonian about a century after Nebuchadnezzar, but fashions must have changed, since this description does not altogether fit with what we see on monuments of the time of that King. Herodotus says that Babylonian men used perfumes, and although we have nothing to give direct confirmation of this for the time of Nebuchadnezzar, there are certainly plenty of recipes for perfume-making known from Assyria from a rather earlier period. The use of scent by Babylonian men did not, of course, imply that they were perverts: it probably arose from the fact that with pigs and dogs serving as the only garbage-removers the atmosphere of the streets must have been a little trying to fastidious nostrils on a muggy day.

How did an average Babylonian actually spend his day? There are of course many details we do not know, but it is possible to put together a general outline in which all the individual facts are authentic. Let us consider a certain Bel-ibni, who was, we may suppose, a skilled goldsmith. Bel-ibni and his wife woke up just before dawn, kissed each other and the children, and then went for a bath, which they completed by rubbing themselves down with olive oil and perfumes. The wife then superintended the slaves in the production of breakfast, whilst Bel-ibni and the boys of the family went on to the roof to prostrate themselves before the rising sun. After breakfast Bel-ibni went along to a small temple near by, taking, for an offering due from him, a lamb which he had bought the previous day and which had been tied up in the courtyard all night. As he entered the temple courtyard he saw a disturbance going on: a man had just been arrested by the temple guards for attempting to approach a certain part of the temple without performing the appropriate ceremonial. Bel-ibni handed over his lamb to a temple official, whose scribe quickly drew up a receipt on a small clay tablet, at the same time entering a note of the source of the lamb on a much larger tablet destined for the temple's annual records. This duty done, Bel-ibni then made his way towards the great city-temple Esagila, passing near the river embankment, where he stopped for a moment to watch the bustle of the shipping. At the quay serving Esagila a foreign ship which had come up from the Persian Gulf was unloading a cargo of ingots of copper; a smaller vessel which had brought a load of alum down from Carchemish was waiting its turn, and another one was being loaded with sesame destined for the temple of one of the cities downstream from Babylon. Leaving the riverside, Bel-ibni made his way to one of the offices within the precincts of Esagila, where the appropriate authorities issued him with a quantity of gold, giving him instructions to make rings and bangles for the adornment of a new statue of Marduk. He was also given a much smaller sum in the form of a strip of silver, which represented payment in advance for his work. Here again, tablets were drawn up, specifying the weights of gold and silver paid to the goldsmith and the work to be done. Bel-ibni now made his way to the goldsmiths' bazaar, stopping on the way at the house of a merchant to buy a *gur* sack (about four bushels) of barley, for which he snipped off and weighed out a piece from his strip of silver; the merchant sent off a slave with the corn to Bel-ibni's house.

As Bel-ibni's day had begun at about five a.m. by our time, it was now still before eight. At his workshop in the goldsmiths'

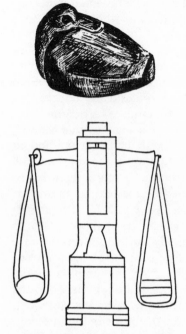

106 Assyrian scales and 'duck' weight

bazaar, Bel-ibni found his oldest son Kudda awaiting him, with the charcoal brazier used for melting the metal already blown into life with bellows. Bel-ibni and his son whispered a short traditional incantation in the name of the patron-god of the goldsmiths, and then placed the gold in a terracotta crucible, and moved the crucible gradually into the hottest part of the charcoal. Bel-ibni's son applied himself, as his father had taught him, to the blowpipe, and soon had the charcoal around the crucible at a white heat. Bel-ibni had meanwhile taken the appropriate moulds from the terracotta box in which he kept his stock-in-trade, and had set these up in a bowl of sand and put the whole lot to heat up, so that the molten metal should not crack the moulds. Finally the gold in the crucible melted, and Bel-ibni took tongs and lifted out the crucible, pouring its molten contents carefully into the moulds. The gold was given time to set and cool off, and the ornaments were then withdrawn from their moulds. With the aid of files, chisels, punches and light hammers, gold and silver wire, solder and heat judiciously applied with the blowpipe, Bel-ibni and his son converted the plain castings into fine examples of Babylonian embossed and engraved ornamentation and filigree work.

They worked on with only an occasional pause, as when they stopped to listen to a crier announcing the details of a runaway slave, or the laments of the womenfolk announced a death in a dwelling near by. When the heat and height of the sun told them that midday was near, Bel-ibni and Kudda packed away their tools and moulds in the tool-chest, carefully banked up the brazier with charcoal and damped it down, probably with a coating of clay, until it was only just smouldering and would remain alight until the evening. They could probably always borrow fire from a neighbour if their brazier did go out, but to do this too often would give a man a bad name for improvidence.

Bel-ibni and Kudda were now able to return home, taking with them for safety the completed ornaments and any scraps of gold left over, for which they would have to account to the temple authorities. On the way home they passed a temple, in the courtyard of which a group of their neighbours was sitting, listening to the details of a lawsuit brought by one man against another about the ownership of a plot of land between their houses. Old men who remembered the fathers of the litigants were just giving evidence of transactions concerning that piece of land supposed to have happened a generation before. In a corner of the courtyard a man sat whimpering in pain whilst a friend bathed with oil a great red weal on his forehead: the man had been found out in forging a clay tablet about a property deal, and his punishment had been to have the tablet heated in a brazier and branded into his forehead.

Bel-ibni and Kudda arrived home to find Bel-ibni's wife in some excitement. The new slave-girl, whom Bel-ibni had only bought a fortnight before, had had an epileptic fit during the morning. This was annoying, as Bel-ibni had thought she was a promising girl as concubine for Kudda, who was fourteen and just becoming interested in such things, but there was no financial loss involved, since the girl carried a three-month guarantee against such symptoms and Bel-ibni had only to return her to get his money back.

Bel-ibni and his wife, Kudda and the younger son and daughter, now had their light lunch around the table in the main room, as already described. Afterwards Bel-ibni and his wife went to their bedroom for the siesta. The heat outside was now intolerable, but within the massive walls of the rooms, with their thick mud roofs and small ventilation openings, the temperature remained quite comfortable. Tired after the work and heat of the morning, Bel-ibni and his wife soon fell asleep. They awoke refreshed and made love: this was not only a pleasure but also a positive duty. Bel-ibni's wife was five months pregnant, and the omen collections stated that this was a highly favourable time for this activity.

Bel-ibni now had another bath, and with Kudda returned for further work in the goldsmiths' bazaar. At dusk they returned home for the main evening meal. Tonight there was a minor festival at the local temple, and so after the meal all the members of the family put on their best clothing, arranged their hair-styles with special care, and went along to join in the festivities. There seems to be no proof that at this period Bel-ibni's wife would have had to be veiled in public, although at earlier periods of Babylonian and Assyrian history this was certainly usual.

The temple courtyard flickered in the light of torches made of reeds soaked in crude bitumen, and there was a great throng of people, most of them neighbours known to Bel-ibni, dancing and singing. In the entrance to the main shrine at one side of the courtyard the priests inspected a bull with its legs tied, all ready for slaughter. Silence fell as they began intoning a long series of ritual texts, many of them quite unintelligible to anyone listening, since they were in the dead language Sumerian. The sense of the ritual was none the less not lost on the crowd, for a group of masked priests performed a series of symbolic fights and dances reflecting the mythological allusions contained in the words of the ritual. As one of the actors fell to the ground in mimic death the crowd would break out in lamentation, or when a god was seen to overcome the evil powers opposing him the watchers broke into cries of joy.

When the festival was at an end, or when Bel-ibni had seen enough, the family returned home again. The slaves had already placed torches in the courtyard and lighted lamps at the entrance of the house and in the main room. Whilst Bel-ibni's wife gave the slaves instructions for the next day's household work, Bel-ibni played with his little daughter and watched his two sons entertaining themselves at a kind of draughts (the rules of which we do not know). A light supper brought the day to an end.

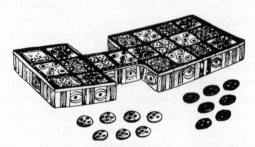

107 Gaming board of 2000 years before Nebuchadnezzar

Chapter IX

RELIGION

IN modern life some people do not recognise the claims of religion at all, whilst some who do accept religion as having a claim on them tend to isolate it as a separate compartment of their lives. These attitudes would have been unthinkable in the ancient world. To ancient man religion was not an optional extra, but rather was the aspect of existence which formed the basis of the whole of life.

In the modern world we try to make clear-cut distinctions between the various categories of fortune-telling, magic, religion, theology, and ethics. Such distinctions are not always easy to maintain even in the modern world, and in ancient times would have been almost meaningless. In the ancient world all these elements were parts of one great whole. It is this whole, not strictly divided into our own categories, to which it is hoped to give some brief introduction here.

Ancient religion, despite the conservatism which was a marked feature of it, did in the course of time undergo changes of emphasis and even of belief and practice. Also, the religion of Assyria was not identical at all points with the religion of Babylonia. For these reasons it is advisable, in discussing ancient Mesopotamian religion, to choose a particular period and place. In what follows most of the statements are based on evidence from Assyria at about 700 B.C., though some evidence from Babylonia and from other periods is included to fill out the picture.

It is necessary to make clear at the outset what it is we are discussing. Apart from a few comments by travellers such as Herodotus (fifth century B.C.), we know nothing of what went on in Babylonian and Assyrian religion except what we find in the cuneiform texts and what we can infer from the architecture of the temples. The cuneiform texts were mostly drawn up and used by particular classes of learned priests, and so for the greatest part are concerned only with official religion. Only by chance do such texts occasionally give some hint about how religious observances affected ordinary people. It is true that the very common magical texts for driving away demons (see below, pp. 186–7) do to some extent bridge the gap between official and popular religion, but even so they only touch the life of the ordinary man at the point at which he was suffering from some particular trouble. Apart from this kind of thing we are very much in the dark as to the religious attitudes of the ordinary illiterate peasants of Babylonia and Assyria. Any picture we can present is therefore likely to be very one-sided. Some conclusions can, however, reasonably be drawn.

We should be wrong, in thinking of how religion affected the ordinary Babylonian or Assyrian, to begin by analysing the list of gods who were supposed to control the universe and its various compartments. Gods there were, thousands of them, but the ordinary man was probably actively concerned with only five or six of them at the most. These would of course be the ones who helped him in his daily life, particularly those who protected him from the attacks of demons, from witchcraft, and from injustice a the hands of his fellow-men, or who could warn him of impending dangers.

There was a great deal of superstition in the life of the ancient people of Babylonia, as indeed there still is in the life of modern people. However, one notable difference between superstition in the ancient world and in our own times is that now it is condemned by official religion. In the ancient world superstition, far from being condemned by official religion, was a part of religion itself.

One of the most prominent aspects of ancient superstition was the belief in demons. From the point of view of the average Assyrian or Babylonian, there might be demons almost anywhere, though there were some places and circumstances which they particularly favoured. They were especially likely to be found in the desert, which was why the desert was such a dangerous place to wander around in. Graveyards and ruined buildings were other favoured lurking places. Demons were likely to be particularly active when a woman was expecting or had just had a child— hence, in the ancient way of thinking, the high rate of child-bed fever and infant mortality. Most illnesses were put down to their direct interference, and they were likely to try to take up residence in a newly built house, to the harm and inconvenience of the human owners. Not all spirits were ill-disposed: some served to protect human beings, and the colossal bulls and lions which were placed

108 Moving a colossal bull

outside Assyrian palaces (*4, 108*) represented protecting spirits of this kind.

The origin of the harmful demonic powers was of various kinds. Some were said to have been 'spawned by the great god Anu', others had their origin in the Underworld, and yet others were ghosts of human beings. Some of the demons of divine origin were powerful enough to interfere not only with human beings but even with the gods themselves, a notable instance being at eclipses of the moon. A text relates that 'the seven evil gods [a particular group of demons] forced their way into the vault of heaven; they clustered angrily round the crescent of the Moon-god'. In the particular text from which this comes, the gods themselves dealt with the matter. In practice, however, men also had their part to play when this happened, and they helped to drive off the demons causing eclipses by means of a special sacred kettle-drum which was set up in the temple courtyard and beaten. Such is human conservatism that this ceremony still went on even after the Babylonians knew what caused eclipses and could calculate them accurately in advance.

The way in which demons manifested themselves and came to interfere in human activities, and the manner in which their ill effects could be overcome, may be best shown by quoting a few texts out of many possible examples.

Demons are frequently described as being seven in number:

Seven are they! In the mountains of the west were they born.
Seven are they! In the mountains of the east did they grow up.
In caves of the earth do they dwell,
In waste places of the earth do they suddenly appear.
. . . .
The seven of them go running over the mountains of the west;
The seven of them go dancing over the mountains of the east.

Another text describes the demons more exactly:

Amongst the seven of them, one is the south wind (in the form of)
    a dragon,
The second is a dragon with open mouth,
The third is a fierce leopard . . .,
The fourth is a great viper . . .,
The fifth is a raging lion whose spring cannot be avoided,
The sixth is [description lost],
The seventh is a whirlwind . . .

This 'seven' represented simply one class of demons; there were other species in addition to these. One of the nastiest demons was one known as Lamashtu, a female who tried to steal newborn babies from their mothers (*109*).

The demons could take all kinds of forms, as well as their own proper shapes(*110*). They could lie down in the form of an ass to wait for a man to approach, or run about the city at night in the shape of a fox, or go around in packs like hounds, or slither along the ground like snakes. Ordinary protective measures had little effect upon demons, as they could creep into a house through a crack in the door or blow in like a draught. They were capable of unbelievably swift movement, and are described as flitting past like shooting stars.

109 The demon Lamashtu

It was not only demons who were likely to harm people. There were also evilly disposed humans who, as witches or wizards, were capable of inflicting sickness or misfortune upon a person by means of spells. Fortunately, these evil powers, whether demonic or human, could generally be overcome by magical means, and a whole class of priest-magicians existed ready (for a fee) to provide their assistance.

The following is a fairly typical kind of text setting out what a priest-magician (or *mashmashu*, as he was called in the Akkadian language) was to do in the case of a particular type of sufferer. The man concerned seems to have been troubled with what we might call a serious neurosis, which gave him a feeling of being haunted and in bad health. The text says:

> If a ghost has seized a man and persecutes him, or a . . . demon has seized him, or an Evil Thing has grasped his hand and will not be

110 The demon Pazazu

separated from him, you shall take dust from a ruined town, a ruined house, a ruined temple, a grave, a neglected garden, a neglected canal, and a disused road, and you shall mix it with bull's blood and make an image of the Evil Thing. You shall clothe it with a lion's skin, and thread a carnelian stone and put it round its neck. You shall make it hold a leather bag, and you shall supply it with provisions. . . . You shall make it stand on the roof of the sick man's house. You shall . . . pour out (a libation). You shall set up three cedar-wood posts at its sides [to form a tripod over it]. You shall surround it with a circle of flour. Towards sunset you shall cover it with a . . . pot in which nothing has been cooked. [This was presumably inverted over the tripod.] . . . For three days the *mashmashu* shall . . . by day set out an incense burner with gum-juniper before Shamash [the Sun-god], by night heap up emmer flour before the stars of night. Before Shamash and the stars he shall then, for three days, recite for the sick man:

'Evil Thing, from this day from the body of So-and-so son of So-and-so you are separated, cast forth, . . . and chased away. The god or goddess who put you (there) has separated you from the body of So-and-so the sick man.'

On the third day towards sunset you shall set up the offering equipment before Shamash. The sick man shall raise the image before Shamash and repeat thus:

Incantation: 'O Shamash, . . . judge of heaven and earth, . . . who establishes light for the people; Shamash, when you set, light is withdrawn from the people. . . . When you come forth, all mankind becomes warm. The cattle and living things that go out on the steppe-land, they come towards you, you give them life. You judge the case of the wronged man and wronged woman; you give them a just decision. I, So-and-so son of So-and-so, kneel full of trouble, because a curse binds me, . . . (because) shivering, dizziness, diseased flesh, vertigo, arthritis, disordered mind have weighed me down, make me moan every day. . . . Judge my case, give a decision for me, making a decision (in my favour). . . .'

Thus you shall make him say. You shall put it [the image] in the pot and you shall put it under a curse and say:

'You are accursed by the oath of the heavens, You are accursed by the oath of Shamash.'

You shall (then) seal its mouth [*i.e.* the mouth of the pot], . . . and you shall bury it in deserted wasteland.

There are various disputable features in this text but the main principles seem clear. The demon interfering with the man was induced to take up residence in the image made of dust and bull's blood, and magical steps (in the form of the lion skin, the red jewel and the magic circle of flour) were taken to ensure that it could not afterwards escape. Demons were apparently immortal and could not be actually destroyed, but they could be buried out of harm's way.

The tablet from which the foregoing text is taken contains several other rituals, all with the same basic purpose though with different details. One of these texts gives away the fact that the *mashmashu* was not always successful in his treatment, for it begins: 'If the hand of an *utukku*-demon has seized a man, and the *mashmashu* is unable to remove it. . . .'

A feature of Babylonian and Assyrian demons seems to have been their unsuspecting nature and low intelligence. They could very easily be tricked or deceived. They could, as we have seen, be trapped in a pot or an image; alternatively, they could be induced to transfer their attentions to an animal or an image or even a stick which by magical means was substituted for the victim they had been plaguing.

111 Shamash, the Sun-god

187

Most of the foregoing has been concerned with demons properly speaking, that is, beings of a special category between men and gods. Technically distinct from these, but often much the same in their practical effect, were the ghosts of dead humans. The proper place for ghosts was, of course, the Underworld. The Underworld in ancient Mesopotamian thought was not a very inviting conception (p. 198), but at least the ghost of a person who was properly buried and who received the proper grave offerings found repose there. The trouble arose with ghosts of people who had died violent deaths, or whose bodies had not received proper treatment after death. Such ghosts, full of malevolence to living humans, could wander around and cause illness, nightmares, or disorders of the mind, in much the same way as the demons. Many of the exorcisms include ghosts alongside demons in the list of possible causes of the trouble, though other rituals single out ghosts for special treatment.

Not all ghosts were considered harmful to mankind. The ghost of a person decently buried and properly provided with funerary offerings was potentially well-disposed, and, being in touch with the authorities of the Underworld, could usefully be invoked on behalf of his still living kindred, as in the following extract from a long ritual:

You, the ghosts of my family, . . .
As many as lie at rest in the (Under)world, I have made a funerary
    offering to you;
I have poured out water for you; . . .
Stand before Shamash and Gilgamesh today!
Judge my case! Decide the details of the decision about me!
The Bad Thing which is in my body, in my flesh, in my veins,
Appoint over to the hand of Namtar, Messenger of the
    (Under)world; . . .
Seize him [*i.e.* the Bad Thing] and send him down to the Land of
    No Return!
Let me, your servant, live, let me prosper.
Because of the magical rites let me be ritually clean in your name.
I will give cold water for your wraith to drink.
Give life to me that I may utter your praise.

Magical rituals like those referred to above, though most common in connection with demons (or ghosts) and the illnesses and misfortunes thought to have been caused by them, could also be used in rather different circumstances. If for example a man had the unpleasant experience of a dog cocking its leg against him (and there have always been plenty of ill-mannered dogs around Oriental cities), this was an omen of very bad misfortune in store. However, just as with us, if a person spills salt, the misfortune this supposedly foretells can be prevented by throwing some salt over the shoulder, so with the dog-soiled Babylonian gentle-

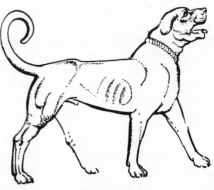

112 A Babylonian dog

man, his coming disaster could be prevented by the appropriate ritual. A text gives full details as to what was to be done by a *mashmashu* to put things right:

> *Ritual for it.* You shall make a dog of clay. You shall put a piece of cedar-wood at its neck. You shall pour oil on its head. You shall coat it with goat-hair. . . . You shall make a bonfire for Shamash on the bank of the river. You shall arrange twelve loaves of emmer bread . . . [and other food and drink offerings]. . . . You shall set up an incense burner of gum-juniper. You shall pour a libation of best quality beer. You shall make the man kneel down. You shall take up that image and say thus:
> *Incantation:* 'O Shamash, king of heaven and earth. . . .'

The incantation mentions the trouble and concludes:

> 'Set the evil of that dog far away,
> That I may praise you!'

The instructions continue:

> Thus it shall be said before Shamash. Over that image you shall say thus:
> 'I give you as my substitute.
> Let the evil destined for my body be upon you. . . .
> Let the evil before and behind me be upon you.'
> When you have said this, you shall go away from Shamash and turn to the river and say:
> *Incantation:* 'This dog has sprinkled me with urine. I am afraid

189

and fearful. Let this evil not return to its place (on the earth), . . . let it not be near. . . .'

    Incantation: 'Let that dog be far off in the Abyss. . . . Extract from my body the evil (omen) of the dog; grant me to live happily.'

    Thus you shall say three times. You shall throw that image into the river. He [the man who met the dog] shall not look behind him. He shall go to the tavern.

The text about the omen from the dog's misconduct illustrates one of the great pseudo-religious preoccupations of the ancient people of Mesopotamia. The course of events was believed to be in the hands of the divine powers, and things happened because the gods had decided that they should. If the gods already knew what was going to happen, it was a reasonable assumption that in some circumstances they would give a glimpse of future events to human beings. Out of this way of looking at things there grew up a great pseudo-science devoted to the obtaining and interpretation of omens.

From our point of view, a useful distinction can be made between omens drawn from chance happenings, such as treading on a lizard, and omens deliberately obtained by slaughtering a sheep to examine its internal organs, particularly the liver. Artificially obtained omens were especially favoured in State circles, in which connection their use has been referred to elsewhere (pp. 62–63). Another form of fortune-telling used particularly in State circles, which rivalled liver-divination in antiquity and finally superseded it in popularity, was astrology. At about the time and period with which we are mainly concerned at present (700 B.C. in Assyria) reports were regularly made to the King about the appearance of the moon and planets, with comments upon what these things foretold. The application of astrology to individuals, in the form in which (most regrettably) many of our own newspapers and journals still pander to this superstition, had to await the invention of the twelve signs of the zodiac, which took place in Babylonia soon after 500 B.C.

One of the less artificial types of fortune-telling, in vogue not only in ancient Mesopotamia but throughout the whole ancient Near East, was divination by dreams. Everyone is familiar with the stories in the Bible about dreams which Joseph had as a boy (*Genesis* xxxvii 5–10) and those which later on he interpreted in Egypt (*Genesis* xl 5–19, xli 1–32). This kind of thing is very well known also from outside the Bible, and there are several records of dreams of Egyptian, Hittite and Mesopotamian kings, most of them quite transparent in meaning. There are also 'Dream Books' written on cuneiform tablets, giving long lists of dreams and their meanings.

There are other long compilations containing lists of omens drawn from accidental occurrences, such as the birth of an abortion or misshapen baby, or from random events of everyday life, such as an unusual bird sitting on a housetop.

It is appropriate here to give some brief account of the nature of some of the gods whose intentions the Babylonians and Assyrians were so anxious to know. No attempt will be made to catalogue all the gods whose names are known, since they run into thousands, most of them of importance only in particular places or at particular periods or in connection with particular activities.

At the head of the pantheon were three great gods, Anu, Enlil and Ea (or Enki, to give him his original Sumerian name). Anu was nominally king of the gods, but from early Sumerian times he had become a rather shadowy figure, and was first associated with, and afterwards in practice superseded by, Enlil. Enlil, whose name is Sumerian for 'Lord Wind', was the Storm-god. He represented the divine in its transcendent aspect, and though he could be of gracious countenance, the human race crossed him only at their peril. He could be as violent as the storm, and it was he who insisted on the destruction of mankind by the Deluge (p. 92). Ea (Enki) on the other hand, we might call the immanent aspect of deity. He was the god of Wisdom and Magic and was invariably benign. It was he who had established the world order and given mankind the gifts of civilisation; he, too, had prevented the utter destruction of the human race in the Deluge. He it was who was the ultimate source of magical power against the demonic enemies of mankind.

Each of these three great gods had consorts, but none was, in the period with which we are mainly concerned, more than a faint reflection of her husband. Once one leaves the early Sumerian period, the only prominent goddesses one finds are Ereshkigal, queen of the Underworld, so powerful that all the gods were expected to stand up out of respect to her messenger, and Inanna. Inanna, identified with the Semitic goddess Ishtar, had her visible form as the planet Venus, the morning and evening star. She came to absorb many attributes which may originally have belonged to a number of other goddesses, but her major aspects were those

113 Marduk, the national god of Babylonia

of goddess of love and of war. Cults of a sexual nature were carried on in her honour in many places.

Ishtar, as the planet Venus, is often thought of in a group with Sin, the Moon-god, and Shamash, the Sun-god (*111*). Because he saw everything in his daily course above the earth, Shamash was also god of justice. There was a strong moral element in the cult of Shamash, who was an unsparing enemy of the wrongdoer and the oppressor, and a friend of the just and the oppressed. A god often associated with Shamash was Adad, another storm-god, originally of West Semitic origin.

Enlil had been regarded as the old national god of Sumer, and later many of his attributes were taken over by the national gods of Babylonia and Assyria, respectively Marduk (*113*) and Ashur, who played the central part in the State cults of their respective countries.

A Babylonian god who in the later period rivalled Marduk in importance was Nabu, son of Marduk, patron of the city of Borsippa near Babylon, and god of the Scribal Art. Although it has been denied, Marduk and Nabu both seem to have represented (amongst other things) aspects of the Sun-god, Marduk as the sun during the daytime or during the summer, Nabu as the sun at night or at midwinter. Because of this association, an odd little ceremony took place in Babylon twice a year. On midsummer's day, two minor goddesses (known elsewhere as the hairdressers of Marduk's wife) went in solemn procession from Esagila, the temple of Marduk, to Ezida, the temple of Nabu. At midwinter, when the night was longest and about to shorten, the two goddesses went in the reverse direction, from Nabu's temple to Marduk's. A cuneiform text explains the purpose of this:

In the month of Tammuz [June], when the nights are short, in order
to lengthen the nights the daughters of Esagila go to Ezida. Ezida is
the Night House. In the month of Tebet [December], when the days
are short, the daughters of Ezida, in order to lengthen the days, go
to Esagila. Esagila is the Day House.

Two other major gods who should be mentioned were Ninurta
and Nergal. Ninurta, a son of Enlil, was a warrior god, and was
particularly reverenced in Assyria. Nergal was patron god of the
Babylonian city of Kutha. A myth relates how he became the
husband of Ereshkigal and so king of the Underworld; as such he
was greatly feared. Three other gods whose names quite frequently
occur were Gibil, Gira and Nusku, fire-gods who were invoked
particularly in connection with measures taken against witchcraft.

A god on a different level from all the foregoing was Tammuz,
originally a deified King of early Sumerian times. Lamentation for
his death was the central feature of a popular fertility cult which
spread widely in the Near East, even reaching Jerusalem (*Ezekiel*
viii 14). Some people have even gone so far as to suggest that
Tammuz was a dying god who rose again and who was in consequence the centre of a saviour cult, but there is no evidence at
all for this.

Both amongst the greater and the lesser deities, there was a
constant tendency to reduce their numbers by identifying one with
another. Thus a hymn to the goddess Bawa boldly stated that a
number of other goddesses were only aspects of Bawa:

In Ur, [she is] Ningal, sister of the great gods;

In Sippar, city of ancient times, . . . she is Aya;
In Babylon, . . . she is Eruʾa.

Those named were the principal deities commonly mentioned in
the first millennium B.C., but in addition to them there were hosts
of lesser ones, many of whom were patrons of various trades and
activities. Foreign gods were also recognised, for there was no
narrow exclusiveness in Assyro-Babylonian religious thought.
Assyrian kings referred to the gods of their vassals and even called
upon them to wreak vengeance upon those who failed to observe
treaty obligations. We find Esarhaddon, in his treaty with the vassal
King of Tyre, expressing the wish that in the event of default by
the Tyrian,

Bethel and Anath-Bethel may deliver you into the power of a ravenous lion. . . . Baal-sameme, Baal-malage, (and) Baal-zephon may make a foul wind come upon your ships, and may loosen their structure and tear out their masts, so that a great wave may sink them in the sea.

All the great gods were originally associated with particular cities, where their cult was always specially held in honour. Thus Anu was associated with Erech, Enlil with Nippur, Enki (Ea) with Eridu, Inanna (alongside Anu) with Erech, Marduk with Babylon, and so on. The cult of a god was not limited to his own city, and there were temples or chapels of many different gods in every great city. At festivals, the images of the gods might leave their temples to visit the shrines of other deities. This is well attested for the New Year Festival.

The New Year Festival, the principal religious event of the year throughout Babylonia and Assyria, still presents us with many problems. Our knowledge of it has to be pieced together from evidence relating to several different periods and places, and is still far from complete. In Babylon the festival took place during the first eleven days of the first month, Nisan. The calendar, which was basically lunar, was if necessary adjusted by the insertion of an extra month (p. 64) so that the spring equinox would fall during the New Year Festival.

During the first five days of the festival various ceremonies of purification and preparation were performed. These culminated in the High Priest taking the King in before Marduk, to whom he surrendered his royal insignia. The King received a blow in the face from the High Priest, and was forced to his knees, where he uttered a formula claiming to have been innocent of various offences against Marduk's city. His insignia were then restored to him. On the sixth day the image of the god Nabu arrived from the city of Borsippa, about ten miles away, and entered Esagila, the temple of his father Marduk. The details of what Marduk and Nabu did during the following days we do not know: in general terms it is likely that they were engaged in decreeing the fate of the city for the following year. There may also have taken place at this time a sacred marriage between the King and a high priestess, representing deities.

The climax of the festival took place on the tenth day. The statues of Marduk, Nabu, and other gods, dressed in sacred garments adorned in gold, assembled in the great courtyard of

Esagila, while the people of the city looked on in awed excitement. The procession was then led by the King himself, partly along the roads and partly by barge on the canals, to a building known as the Akitu House. This was a chapel set in the midst of gardens outside the city proper. In the Akitu House some kind of ritual (of which the details are unknown) took place, in which Marduk had a symbolic battle with the monsters representing the forces of chaos. After his victory Marduk and his procession were taken back to the city in triumph, the populace shouting over and over again their ritual cries of joy.

There were lesser festivals at many other times during the year, and to ensure the due performance of the cult of the gods each temple had its own staff of religious personnel, both male and female. There were priests of various classes, from the High Priest downwards, to perform sacrifices and other rituals in which the gods were directly approached. Another group of personnel comprised administrators to look after temple property and ensure the provision of all the material equipment necessary for the cult. Other functionaries included various classes of diviners and exorcists, as well as officiants such as sword-bearers (for slaughtering sacrificial animals), and carpenters and jewellers for making statues or figurines used in certain ceremonies. There were also musicians (*114*) and singers, both male and female. All the men amongst the above-mentioned groups were normally married, and exercised their offices in the temple as an hereditary right, at least in the late period (after 500 B.C.). A share of the temple revenues went with each office and, in the period mentioned, the right to exercise an office in the temple and to enjoy the income from it could be freely bought and sold. This, however, was in the period when Babylonian religion was a spent force: earlier, when it had been in its full vigour, the sale of offices in the temple must have been far less usual, as unsuitable birth or any physical

114 Assyrian musicians

195

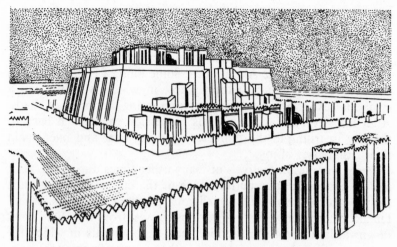

115 A Babylonian temple at Uruk, eighth century B.C.

blemish disqualified a person from exercising any such office. Also, in the earlier period, some offices in the temples were certainly royal appointments.

A word should be said about another group of temple personnel. These were the religious prostitutes, not only women but also men who had been made eunuchs. Ishtar was, as we have said, the goddess of love, and the sexual practices in which these people were concerned were principally in her honour. There is good reason to think that similar practices were at one period carried on in the temple built by Solomon in Jerusalem, though there it met with vigorous opposition from the followers of Yahweh. In Babylonia and Assyria such practices involved no stigma, and it seems that a lady whose duties lay in this sphere might be respectably married.

If the foregoing seems to put the religion of the average Babylonian or Assyrian at a very crude and low level, it is probably not doing the average Babylonian or Assyrian a great injustice. His religion, in many of its features, was low and crude, and we find Isaiah viewing it with amused contempt. None the less, there was a nobler side to it, even if this is not so readily evident. Embedded within some of the magical ritual texts there were prayers to some of the great gods, and although these are labelled 'incantations', so that there must have been some feeling that they operated simply as magical forms of words, their spirit is nobler than this would

196

suggest. Some of them have a definite ethical content, since the god is sometimes described as judging the case of the wronged man or wronged woman. This higher side of religion becomes particularly apparent when we turn to some of the hymns to the great gods. Thus a Babylonian hymn to Shamash refers at length both to the beneficence of the Sun-god and to the moral standards set by him. The worshipper says to the god:

You take care of all the people of the lands;
Everything that Ea, the king, the counsellor, has brought into being
    is wholly entrusted to you.
Whatever has breath, you shepherd equally;
You are their keeper, above and below.

As a definite statement of the Sun-god's ethical standards the worshipper says in the same hymn:

You give the crooked judge experience of prison;
The person who perverts justice for a bribe, you make to bear
    punishment.
He who does not accept a bribe but takes the part of the weak
Is pleasing to Shamash, who will give him long life.

Hymns and prayers of this kind, as well as other texts, show that, as we have said, Babylonian religion had a definite ethical content. Although a Babylonian cynic might express the view that

What (seems) proper to oneself is an offence to a god,
What (seems) despicable in one's own heart is proper to one's god,

the ordinary belief was that there were certain forms of action obviously pleasing to the gods, and others displeasing and liable to incur the gods' wrath.

How were the beliefs of ancient man reflected in his general attitude to life? It is usually said that the ancient Mesopotamian's view of life was essentially pessimistic, by which is meant that the prevalent view was one which regarded human existence as ultimately futile. Although some gods, particularly Shamash, appeared to be motivated by considerations of ethical justice, the ancient myths mostly appeared to teach that the life of man was decided not by righteous gods bound by their own moral laws, but by the arbitrary interplay of the uncertain tempers of the leaders of the

197

pantheon. If the Babylonian or Assyrian saw only futility in his life on earth, he had no compensating hope of a better state beyond the grave, for the Underworld was a place of gloom and dust. It was commonly accepted that mankind had been created for no other purpose than to act as servants for the gods, and therefore there was no reason for an individual man to expect to be of significance in either this world or the next. This attitude was undoubtedly strongly embedded in Mesopotamian thought, but it has been pointed out that this belief about the purpose of man had another side to it. Certainly mankind was, in the Assyro-Babylonian view, merely created to do the service of the gods, but conversely the gods needed the service of mankind in order to continue to exist in the accustomed divine order. In the last resort, the well-being of the gods in heaven, and the maintenance of the created universe, depended upon human society on earth. The individual human had no purpose and no destiny, but the world was unthinkable without the human race.

BOOKS FOR FURTHER READING

Archaeological Background

E. A. T. W. BUDGE, *The rise and progress of Assyriology* (London, 1925, reprinted 1975).
A. H. LAYARD, *Nineveh and its remains*, vol. I and chapters XI–XIV in vol. II (John Murray, 1849), [Copies of this bestselling nineteenth-century work are still sometimes available secondhand. There is an abridged one-volume edition with the same title, edited by H. W. F. Saggs (Routledge & Kegan Paul, 1970)].
Seton LLOYD, *Foundations in the dust. The story of Mesopotamian exploration* (Thames and Hudson, 1980).
Seton LLOYD, *The archaeology of Mesopotamia* (Thames and Hudson, 1978).
David & Joan OATES, *The rise of civilization* (Elsevier-Phaidon, 1976).

The Sumerians

S. N. KRAMER, *The Sumerians: their history, culture, and character* (University of Chicago Press, 1963).
THORKILD JACOBSEN, *Toward the image of Tammuz and other essays on Mesopotamian history and culture*, edited by W.L. Moran (Harvard University Press, 1970). [Some of the essays concern points of Sumerian or Akkadian grammar, but most are stimulating discussions of aspects of Sumerian society or religion].

Mesopotamian civilization as a whole

A. Leo OPPENHEIM, *Ancient Mesopotamia. Portrait of a dead civilization* (University of Chicago Press, revised edition completed by Erica Reiner, 1977).
Nicholas POSTGATE, *The first empires* (Elsevier-Phaidon, 1977).
Georges ROUX, *La Mésopotamie. Essai d'histoire politique, économique et culturelle* (Editions du Seuil, 1985).
H. W. F. SAGGS, *The Greatness that was Babylon* (Sidgwick & Jackson, revised edition 1987).
Wolfram von SODEN, *Einführung in die Altorientalistik* (Darmstadt, 1985).

The Assyrians

A. K. GRAYSON, *Assyrian royal inscriptions*, 2 vols. (Wiesbaden, 1972 and 1976).
H. W. F. SAGGS, *The might that was Assyria* (Sidgwick & Jackson, 1984).

Religion

J. BOTTÉRO, *La religion babylonienne* (Paris, 1952).
S. H. HOOKE, *Babylonian and Assyrian religion* (Blackwell, Oxford, 1962).
Thorkild JACOBSEN, *The treasures of darkness. A history of Mesopotamian religion* (Yale University Press, 1976).
H. W. F. SAGGS, *The encounter with the Divine in Mesopotamia and Israel* (Athlone Press, London, 1978).

Law

G. CARDASCIA, *Les lois assyriennes* (Éditions du Cerf, Paris, 1969).
G. R. DRIVER and Sir John C. MILES, *The Assyrian laws* (Scientia Verlag, Aalen, corrected reprint, 1975).
G. R. DRIVER and Sir John C. MILES, *The Babylonian laws,* 2 vols. (Clarendon Press, Oxford, 1952 and 1955).
A. FINET, *Le code de Hammurapi* (Éditions du Cerf, Paris, 1973).

The scribe, writing and literature

E. CHIERA, *They wrote on clay* (Phoenix Books, University of Chicago Press, 1959 and later).
G. R. DRIVER, *Semitic writing from pictograph to alphabet* Revised edition edited by S. A. Hopkins, London, 1976).
S. N. KRAMER, *From the Poetry of Sumer* (University of California Press, 1979).
W. G. LAMBERT, *Babylonian Wisdom literature* (Clarendon Press, Oxford, 1960).
J. B. PRITCHARD (ed.), *Ancient Near Eastern texts relating to the Old Testament* (Princeton University Press, third edition, 1969).

Trade and economic life

I. M. DIAKONOFF (ed.), *Ancient Mesopotamia: Socio-economic history. A collection of studies by Soviet scholars* (Nauka Publishing House, Moscow, 1969).
E. LIPINSKI, *State and temple economy in the ancient Near East* (Leuven, 1979).

Crafts and industries

R. J. FORBES, *Studies in ancient technology,* vols. I–IX (Brill, Leiden, second edition, 1964–77).
R. PLEINER & J. K. BJORKMAN, *The Assyrian Iron Age. The history of iron in the Assyrian civilization* (Philadelphia, 1974).

Science

M. LEVEY, *Chemistry and chemical technology in ancient Mesopotamia* (Elsevier, Amsterdam and London, 1959).
O. NEUGEBAUER, *The exact sciences in antiquity* (Dover, New York, second edition, 1969). 1962).
O. NEUGEBAUER, & A. J. SACHS, *Mathematical cuneiform texts* (New Haven, 1945).

Art

A. MOORTGAT, *The art of ancient Mesopotamia* (Phaidon, London and New York, 1969).

INDEX

The numerals in **heavy type** refer to the figure-numbers of the illustrations

INDEX

eclipses, 84–7, 184
Eden, Garden of, 17
education, 77, 101, 167
Egypt, 40, 102, 135, 190
Egypt, ally of Assyria, 52
Egypt, invasion of, 50, 52
El Amarna letters, 41
Elam, 30, 137
Elamites, 24, 25, 37
elephants, 102; **55**
En, 28, 29
engineers, 117
Enki, 124, 125, 191, 194; **71**
Enkidu, 87–91
Enlil, 79, 89, 90, 92, 191, 193, 194
Ensi, 29
envelope tablets, 153–4
Epic of Adapa, 94
Epic of Etana, 94, 95
Epic of Gilgamesh, 87–94
epics, 95
Erech (=Uruk), 29, 87, 88, 89, 90, 93, 94, 194
Ereshkigal, 193
Erra, Myth of, 95
Esagila, 157, 163, 166, 177, 192, 193, 194; **90**
Esarhaddon, 49, 50, 51, 118, 193
Eshnunna, 38, 67, 147; **87**
Eshnunna, laws of, 147–50
Etana, 95; **52**
Etemenanki, 156–7, 163; **90**
ethical standards, 197
Euphrates, 27, 30, 37, 38, 44, 56, 69, 92, 163
examinations, 79
exorcists, 195
Ezida, 192, 193, 195

fables, 61
family, 139
farmers, 66
feasts, 59, 97
ferry, 91
fire-beacons, 67
fishing, 94; **105**
flocks of sheep, 66
Flood (*see also* Deluge), 17
food, 59–61, 174–6

forgery, 152
Fox Talbot, William Henry, 25
friezes, 20
furnace, 131

Gadd, Professor C. J., 77
garrisons, 67
geography of Iraq, 27
geometry, 84; **44**
ghosts, 184, 188
Gibil, 193
Gilgamesh, 29, 87–94, 188; **49**
Gilgamesh, Epic of, 87–94
Gimil-Ninurta, 97–8
Gira, 193
glass, 135–6; **80**
goats, 69, 70, 71, 128–9
gods, 182, 191
Goetze, Professor A., 150
gold, 69
goldsmiths, 177–9
governors, 64
grand army, 115
grave offerings, 101
Greeks, 43
Grotefend, G. F., 23, 25
Gudea, 32; **12**
Gurkhas, 115
Gutians, 31, 32

Habur, River, 40, 44
hairdressers, 157, 192
Hammurabi, 37, 38, 39, 56, 65–6, 137, 146, 147, 150, 163; **82**
Hammurabi, laws of, 137–48, 149, 151
Hanging Gardens of Babylon, 158–62; **92**
Haran, 150
harvest, 111, 127
hearth, **100**
heaven, 95
Heaven, Bull of, 90
Helbaek, H., 128
Herodotus, 170, 176, 181
Hincks, E., 25
Hittite laws, 150
Hittites, 39, 40, 41, 42, 43
holidays, 78

203

INDEX

INDEX

207